THE

ULTRA MILE

THE
ULTRA MILE

The Joy, Freedom, and
Opportunities of Running

TIM WILLS

Dedication

This book is dedicated to Chase and Connor.

May you find that in pursuit of your passion lies endless possibility.

ACKNOWLEDGMENTS

A bove all, I would like to thank my wife, Catherine Manley, for your unrelenting support, regardless of the dreams that I choose to pursue. To my family, Bill, Rosanne, Tony, and Tiffany, for your time reading and contributing and the races you've attended and offered support. To Christina Manley, who has always expressed interest and been a support in everything I do since the very beginning. To Javier Tella, for providing insight and further clarity on the overall direction and structure of this book, and to Bethany Wright for your continued assistance with the guidance I've requested. All of your feedback and constant support has helped bring this idea from thought to existence.

To my support crew, for the countless miles you stuck by my side and for your friendship that has proven its value from the start: Catherine Manley, Tony Wills, David Hernandez, Yoesly Carvajal, Chris Hirsch, Alioth Nadchar, Danny Guzman, and Jose Mujica. Thank you for sticking by me when the miles were fun, and especially during those miles that proved to be tough. Thank you for making my dream a reality. Without you all, I would not be standing where I stand, nor would I be the person I've become.

Tim Wills
9825 NE 2nd Ave. #530948
Miami Shores, Fl. 33153

For details, contact gotheultramile@gmail.com

Print ISBN: 978-1-09836-093-1
eBook ISBN: 978-1-09836-094-8

Printed in the United States of America on SFI Certified paper.

First Edition

CONTENTS

PART 1:

Running

"I have no special talent. I am only passionately curious."

—Albert Einstein

CHAPTER 1:

The Freedom of Running

The Definition of Run

Would you believe me if I told you the word *run* will soon officially have the most meanings of any word in the dictionary? The *Oxford English Dictionary* will recognize *run* as having a total of 645 meanings. It occurred to me that if one word has so many meanings, perhaps it couldn't hurt for it to have one more. This isn't a random fact but something that brings a peculiar memory to mind. This story is ironic, to say the least, and dates back to my elementary-school years.

I was in an after-school care program, and had to complete homework before going outside to play with the other kids. I vividly remember lying to my teacher, telling him I had finished my homework for his permission to head outside. I gambled he wouldn't ask for verification, but he did and I lost. Not having my homework completed brought me a light punishment for dishonesty, and I was forced to handwrite the definition of run, as he explained it was one of the longest definitions in the dictionary. This moment was a brief glimpse of the lifestyle I would come to love, the very one that would become so engrained within me.

The irony lies in the fact that roughly thirty years later, this publication contains my unique meaning or definition of *run*. I cannot see what is more fitting for a running book than what this very word means to me. So, I write this book to describe the many miles run on foot. Each step taken and every mile run has sculpted my character into who I've become. In a very bizarre way, I continue to write the definition of *run* and exactly what that word means to me.

What Defines a Runner?

There are many definitions and meanings of the word run, so it's perfectly understandable to ask what defines a runner. Luckily for everyone, myself included, there isn't distinct criteria that defines a runner. It can be as subjective and unique as the number of runners that exist. It isn't a specific distance, or even a distinct pace, that classifies someone as a runner. It is more a self-declaration that you are a runner when you intrinsically agree with the statement. Whether you want to complete your first official race, or you occasionally go for a casual jog, it's your call on when you consider yourself a runner.

To this day, I can recollect defining moments when I began to view myself as a runner. My wife, Catherine, who was my girlfriend at the time, was training for the Miami Half-Marathon with her friends and a local running club. She invited me to join her one Saturday morning, and mentioned they were running seven miles that day. I thought to myself, *I've never run seven miles before ....* I agreed, although I don't remember how obvious my reluctance was. In any case, we showed up to run with her group of friends. That didn't go quite as planned, at least not for me.

I had researched on the Internet that, when it came to running long distances, it was recommended that I run slowly. Well I didn't want to screw that up, so I ran slowly... and wasn't able to keep up with my girlfriend or her friends ... or anyone in the group for that matter. After a long and painful seven miles, I strolled back to the group dead last. Everyone was enjoying refreshments and rehydrating. I could hear the group's chatter and laughter. I had struggled to return at all. The run was challenging and, as the miles went on, I began to doubt that I could complete it entirely. Nonetheless, I made it, regardless of how bad I looked when I strolled up to reunite with the group.

I began running a few times per week on my own and meeting up with the group on Saturdays for a long run. The end of January rolled around and we all met at the starting line of the Miami Half-Marathon. Catherine and I ran together, and I will never forget how joyous it was to cross that finish line. When we finished that race, I remember specifically stating that next year I wanted to run the full marathon. I had absolutely no clue how to train for one, and didn't know much at all about running for that matter. However, I was determined from that point forward. More than ten years have passed since that first official finish, and I have not missed a Miami Marathon or Half Marathon since. Aside from that, I am still on a quest to see just what is the furthest distance I can possibly run.

What defines me as a runner today is different than my initial recollections and defining moments. My desire to grow with the sport of running persists. Its evolution from how it began to what it has become goes well beyond initial expectations. Running has found its way deep within me. The sport quickly shifted from an initial interest to more of a long-lasting lifestyle.

The Lifestyle of Running

The sport of running hasn't ever been a hobby of mine or a means of maintaining my fitness levels. It literally became my lifestyle, and it happened as quickly as I can remember. Just as someone whose lifestyle includes traveling the world might ask themselves, *Where do I want to travel next?* that is what it is like for me as a runner. Each and every year I plan what races I am going to run, devise a training plan, and get to work. Excitement stems not only from the previous goals accomplished, but the thoughts of setting new ones and continuing to develop as a runner. I train roughly four to six months for a race, and follow that with a break for recuperation purposes. That break may be weeks or it may be a month. I allot myself time for mental and physical recovery, and then repeat the process of training.

It trickles into more than just training and running races. The majority of my dresser drawers are filled with running apparel and training clothes. All of my socks are running socks. The type of underwear I choose for the day depends on the answer to the question, *Am I running today?* I have a large, three-drawer storage container filled with hydration packs, a surplus of hand-held hydration bottles, blinking lights and head lamps, reflective vests, multiple running watches, new and expired energy gels, electrolyte pills, adhesive bandages, anti-chafing materials, and so on and so forth. I record each mile I run and tally them up each year. I have kept a record of how many miles I run from the beginning of this lifestyle to this day. Furthermore, I also have the tendency to think, read, and write about running.

Before you jump to the conclusion that running is my life, it would be ideal to acknowledge the difference between it being my life, and it being my lifestyle. I get most of my running and training done in my spare time. Believe it or not, no matter how busy we are, we all come across some spare time. It all depends what we choose to do with it. I try to live a balanced lifestyle, which those who know me can attest. I have a beautiful wife and two children, and I juggle work, school, and time with family and friends. It's easy to conclude there may not be time for the enjoyment of running, but I think everyone has some leisure time. There are some who have more time than others, but I think everyone has a type of lifestyle in one form or another.

I have stuck with running for the past ten years and would have it no other way. Out of all the lifestyles to choose from, I would choose no other. I am thirty-seven years old and feel that I'm getting healthier and healthier with age. I feel proud to wear a shirt from a race that tells a story, the struggle it took to earn that finish. And yes, I feel proud when I see my finisher medals hanging in the office of my home. I am proud to be a runner, and would have it no other way!

Is Running Artistic?

The art of running is simple to describe if you've watched elite Olympic marathon runners. Their bodies glide through the air at less than a five-minute-per-mile pace for a distance of 26.2 miles. With such intense effort, it appears so delicate. How a human body sustains performance at this caliber is nothing short of magical. I'm awe-stricken when I try to comprehend the complexity. This is the art of running at its finest.

However, I am asking a different question, whether or not running is artistic. Art can be described in many ways and from a variety of different angles. Late in a race, when all of my mechanics have faltered and my run is described more like a trudge, it certainly doesn't look or appear very artistic. Yet I would like to entertain this idea from another perspective, because my description of artistic is the ability to be expressive through creativity and imagination.

Running is my lifestyle and the means through which I challenge myself. To convey that message through words on these pages not only requires creativity and imagination but it's how I choose to express myself. How does this translate to actually running? I allow my imagination to run wild, without restriction, as it tends to ask permission for challenges I don't believe are possible. Once my imagination and my reality have compromised and arrived at an agreement, it takes a large amount of creativity to actually deliver the accomplishment itself. After all, what I agreed to is just out of reach of what I even believe is possible.

To devise a training plan takes experience and some understanding of the science to apply it. How to develop a plan to get where my imagination wants me to go takes creativity, and it, too, begins from a blank document. To pencil in a series of workouts over a certain duration of time, balance it around life that includes work, school, traveling, family, and friends, and still arrive safely at a starting line my imagination brought me to is inventive. To maximize training and avoid injury, to balance life with lifestyle, and make imagination a reality is considered artistic. I believe we are all artists in our own unique ways, and it all amounts to our method of how we express ourselves to the world around us.

What Do You Think About When You Run?

I am frequently asked, "What do you think about when you run?" It's tough to answer, but I have given this question some thought. When I am running in a relaxed state, it's time to allow my mind to wander freely. I have my own undivided attention, as running without all the daily distractions offers mental freedom. Where does my mind take me, and how can I utilize this time produc-tively?

Running is a way to process the day, whether constructing the one ahead or reflecting upon the one before. Sometimes it can be an opportunity to be mindful of the present moment and simply use it as a form of connection with myself. Think about how much of the day is spent serving the boss, the spouse, the children, and the family. It is equally important to balance our commit-ments, obligations, and responsibilities as it is to invest in our own mental and physical wellbeing.

I think about my wife, Catherine, and my boys, Chase and Connor. Parent-ing has been one of the most rewarding, and at the same time most challenging, aspects of my life. How can I be a better father to them, and how could I be a better husband? What am I proud of? How can I improve upon where I fall short? I think about how happy my boys are when they see me walk through the door and what I can do to increase that happiness. I ponder what lessons I can teach them and what the best possible approach may be. Parenting leaves me more puzzles than I have answers for, and upon reflection I see how I could have handled situations better. I get time to process this information, time I wouldn't have otherwise.

When I place science aside, the subjects of philosophy and critical thinking are my favorite. Both have much to do with deep thought, and what better time to analyze current situations I'm personally baffled by than when I'm running? Life is full of obstacles, troublesome times, and dilemmas to face. Running has provided me with ample time to weigh my options and probabilities to achieve the best outcome. If not during a run, when else would I have an undistracted hour during my whirlwind of a day to properly think about how to handle certain circumstances? I then have a grasp on how to approach these conun-drums in ways I wouldn't have otherwise.

Some of my best thoughts and ideas have sprung up during a run. When I follow through with these thoughts and ideas, it's apparent just how effective this leisure time can be. In fact, the idea of writing this book, in addition to most of its content, was developed during training runs for a race across the state. Running has carved and sculpted the decisions I make in my day-to-day life. Never would I have predicted that the construction of my thoughts while running would be so advantageous. It is considered profitable, and I wish I could quantify the direct impact mental freedom has had on my life.

Everything we do requires a reallocation of our time and energy, which is why balance is one of the most important aspects in our lives. It may seem frantic to achieve and maintain balance, as if a constant force of push and pull is acting upon us. I strive for excellence as much as possible between parenting, work, school, and visits with family and friends. I have not begun to mention where running might fit in, as time management seems to be the only hope in making it all possible within a twenty-four-hour window. It is why we must find our ever-shifting balance in life and right ourselves steadily.

CHAPTER 2:

The Form of Running

Posture and Balance

There is a correlation between the maintenance of posture and our ability to maintain balance. Movement such as running constantly challenges our ability to align our center of gravity within our base of support. No matter where motion takes place, it must be counter balanced elsewhere. Any deviation from the optimal alignment of our bodies, and additional work (energy) is required to negate that action.

An entire textbook can be written in regard to our biomechanics. It is an overwhelming amount of science to digest and just as challenging to apply. However, it's vital to educate ourselves with the basics in order to increase our postural awareness. Being equipped with this content on a superficial level of how our bodies should be positioned will contribute not only to our efficiency but to the preservation of our joints over time.

The key for postural and joint alignment begins with the tilt of our heads. Looking up and forward will set the tone for the entire vertebral column in one form or another. It's important to run tall and align your head centered over the body. An adult head weighs approximately ten to twelve pounds, and the outward positioning needed to look down at the feet requires more strain and energy from the neck and back muscles for stabilization. This can begin to fatigue the cervical and back musculature, causing even more disruption to our overall posture.

The shoulders play an important role, as a common mistake is elevating, or hiking them up, toward the ears. This stores tension in the upper back (trapezius) muscles, requiring, again, more energy and unnecessary strain. Relaxing them down to their lowest level also reminds the entire arm and hands to follow suit. In regard to the shoulders, it's important to avoid a kyphotic posture (hunching) of the upper back, as this could be reduced by slightly retracting the scapula (shoulder blades) together. The best running posture is head up, with the shoulders low and slightly retracted, if necessary.

The arms are not only utilized for momentum but play a crucial role maintaining balance. The arm swing is the reciprocal reaction of our legs. The swing of the arm during push off from the toe can propel the runner forward through momentum as well as maintain balance throughout that propulsion. It helps to maintain approximately a ninety-degree angle or less at the elbow, and to carry a loosely clenched fist. Avoid crossing the midline with each arm swing, as this can begin to tamper with the contralateral (opposite side) pelvis and hip rotation. The relationship between the arms and legs are continuously stabilized and controlled from the torso, also known as the core, which consists of the abdominals, obliques, chest, and back. It is the central link connecting the upper and lower limbs (kinetic chains) as they work in unison.

Perhaps one of the most important aspects of posture and balance while running is having a strong and stable core. A strong torso with an engaged core can increase balance and stability, prevent form breakdown, maintain a neutral pelvis, and thus prevent injury. The running form is but one piece of the puzzle. This is something that can be improved in time, and should become more habitual through awareness, practice, and repetition. It takes time for the postural muscles to develop the memory, and the brain itself finds interest in performing repetitive tasks more efficiently.

Center of Gravity, Base of Support

In keeping with the theme of balance, the hip, knee, and ankle kinetic chain drives the human body forward in some of the most fascinating ways. A kinetic chain is a way to describe human movement, with a notion that each joint or segment has a direct effect on its neighboring joints and, therefore, motion will create a chain of events. It happens not only through the reciprocal arm/leg swing, or the delivery of muscle power but by utilizing a constant force called gravity from an advantageous standpoint.

In anatomical position, body upright and facing the observer, feet flat and palms facing forward, the center of gravity lies anterior to the sacrum. Since humans do not remain fixed in anatomical position when introducing movement, let us assume that, while running, the center of gravity lies within the hip/pelvic region. To maintain stability and balance, the center of gravity must be maintained within the base of support. Picture one foot planted on the ground, providing a base for the weight of the body. The direction of gravity is constant and acts in a downward direction toward the base. Visualize an imaginary line of gravity passing through the center of gravity and base of support. The alignment of our center of gravity and base of support is the key component to maintaining balance and stability.

When the foot comes into contact with the ground, it creates a new base of support. The foot is fixed, and the talocrural joint (ankle) glides about as the weight of the body passes over the center of that base. The moment the center of gravity anticipates passage outside the base of support, another stride will be in transition to provide a new base of support. Running is a balancing act, as the center of gravity is fully reliant on a new base of support in constant formation. Since the feet and ankles provide this all-important base of support and they are relied on heavily to stabilize the body's weight throughout motion, why not invest well in shoe selection and proper footwear? This is precisely the reasoning shoe selection is both complex and subjective, but could be argued as one of the best investments made toward the health of a running career.

A Pair of Running Shoes

Ground reaction force is the force exerted by the ground on the body when they are placed in contact. The ground reaction force placed on the body upon impact can be upward of approximately two-and-a-half times the body weight itself. This immense stress is redistributed through the ankles, knees, hips, and even the back. This is where gait analysis and running shoes enter the equation. Gait analysis is the observational method used to identify possible biomechanical abnormalities. Basically, it's important to know where your foot is landing, how your foot lands, and any biomechanical malalignments that take place within the knees or ankles. These are some factors that should be taken into consideration prior to purchasing a pair of running shoes.

Pronation, the way the foot rolls inward for impact distribution, is a natural movement of the foot and is a desirable component of the gait cycle. Most runners tend to over pronate, which means that upon impact the foot rolls inward, transferring weight to the inner edge, and is commonly seen in those with a lower arch. A stability shoe may offer correction to reduce strain or overuse at the ankle joint. Under pronation, also known as supination, is when the outer edge of the foot strikes the ground at a greater than normal angle. A neutral shoe will allow the foot more freedom to pronate and can offset the original mechanics. Neutral pronation is when the foot lands on the outer edge and rolls inward in a controlled manner, distributing the weight evenly.

Local running stores not only offer a wide selection of the latest models of running shoes but usually provide gait analysis by a knowledgeable staff member who could select several running shoes based on your personal gait pattern. They have been trained to analyze these gait patterns and make specific recommendations for you depending on whether a correction is necessary or not. One of the most frequent questions I receive from people is what kind of running shoes I recommend. My answer is always the same. Go to your nearest running store and take advantage of the gait analysis they offer. Allow them to make several recommendations for you. Try on several different pairs of shoes until one agrees with you. Walk around in them, then jump on the treadmill and do some running at different speeds. The shoe that agrees with your foot the most may very well be the right shoe for you.

Everyone has a different foot. Furthermore, everyone may run a slightly different way. Some runners have a high arch, while others have a low arch. Some runners have no arch at all. Some pronate and some supinate. Some runners have a neutral pronation or have trained themselves to run a specific way to reduce risk of injury. There are those who also need to take previous injury into consideration. Additionally, each runner's goals can vary with regard to speed and distance, in which case each may require a completely different shoe type. Our feet are very specific to us, so running shoes are not a one-size-fits-all approach.

In regard to sizing, each brand differs slightly. Some brands run small, meaning a certain size may feel too tight when compared with another brand of the same size. There are some shoes with a wider than usual toe box to accommodate those with a wider foot. I wouldn't recommend choosing shoes that are too tight, as that wouldn't leave room for any foot swelling during distance runs, nor will it feel good if the toes are constantly jamming the front end of the shoe. If there's too much room within the shoe and the foot has space to shift and slide, that friction can cause the skin to break down and inevitably lead to blistering. While some suggest going up a half size, that may not always be the best solution. Like I previously said, some shoes run small and some run large. To go up a half size on a shoe that already has spare room may not be the right decision, but if you're within your appropriate range then your preference of shoelace tightness will take care of the rest and can be modified to a snug fit.

The life of a running shoe can be a couple hundred miles, and also depends on the shoe and how far you want to stretch them. I would recommend getting a new pair when the bottom tread has worn on the strike points. Not only is this a beneficial indicator to when you need a new pair of shoes but it also shows how you run and where you land. My recommendation of a new pair is not solely due to the tread wear but because the shock-absorption pads within the shoe are likely to have worn as well by this point in time. The lifespan of a running shoe isn't necessarily contingent upon how it looks as a whole but by the areas that are most protective against where we initially strike against a surface. Remember, the ground reaction force is primarily transmitted through where we initially strike, therefore a shoe that is worn out in those particular areas can become purposeless as far as protection is concerned.

CHAPTER 3:

The Joy of Running

The Treadmill Makes a Runner and the Runner Breaks a Treadmill

One day during training, I went to my local gym to hop on the treadmill to do some speed work. I usually did a warm-up mile, followed by another three miles with pace increases each quarter mile. At the time I was training for a five kilometer (5K) race, and used these workouts to increase my anaerobic strength. I did my warm-up mile, and then I increased my pace to where I preferred to initiate the workout. I then increased my pace by about fifteen seconds every quarter mile, such that the next three miles brought me to my overall desired pace.

I raised the pace each quarter mile as the workout dictated I should, regardless of the lactate accumulation beginning to build within my muscles. I remember an odd clicking sound start. I knew it couldn't be good, but just thought that the treadmill was going to need some maintenance soon. My quarter mile repeats continued and so did the noise, which grew increasingly louder. I just wanted to finish my workout, as the feeling of muscle burn and hyperventilation was getting to levels beyond uncomfortable. I was getting close to the end of the workout, and though I contemplated stopping to use another treadmill, the thought of abruptly halting my pacing to change machines only to ramp up the speed again was completely out of the question. Well, not adhering to the warning cries of a machine in distress was a mistake I still laugh about today.

I had just about finished the workout, as I had less than a quarter mile to run. Exhaustion had set in long ago and the pace was just about intolerable at this point. I pictured the track in my mind and knew I literally had less than half a lap to go. The visualization was rudely interrupted by a loud snapping sound, and the belt I was running on suddenly became more slack than snug. It suddenly became unstable and, just as I was about to press the stop button, it began smoking underneath me. I slammed that red button and jumped off the machine as fast as I was running. I told the young worker behind the front counter what happened, completely out of breath and obviously distraught. He printed a simple "Do Not Use" on plain white paper and taped it to the machine. I hopped on another treadmill and got that last quarter mile in at my progressive pace to conclude my workout.

When I was finished and headed to the locker room for a shower, I ironically thought to myself how I wasn't the only one to feel the burn of that workout. I know it could have been coincidence, as the treadmill and I have both shown each other what we can tolerate during previous battles. Coming from the locker room and heading for the exit, I couldn't help but pass the multiple rows of treadmills. Approaching the one that had broken under me, I paused a second to find my pen and couldn't help smiling. I put my ball-point pen to the sign with a grin from ear to ear, and wrote across the paper "You Got Smoked!"

I will always contemplate whether I would have given up first if the treadmill held up a little while longer. We were both trying to survive that workout, but in the end that last quarter mile is always a bit more than expected. I relate this to those last two tenths of a mile during a marathon, which can never be counted out or forgotten. Like that treadmill, I've had the occasional breakdown between miles 26 and 26.2. Those last tenths of a mile must always be provided the respect they deserve. They can cause complete breakdown, and the reason for not accomplishing a time goal or personal best. It's hard to imagine, but what could seem like such a short distance could be where the breaking point lies for a runner, or a treadmill for that matter. In any case, if something had to give that day, I'm certainly glad it was the treadmill and not my ambition.

The Marathon

It took running 26.2 miles to ignite the flame I currently have within, a fire that only seems to grow brighter with time and purpose. It was this distance in particular that introduced me to the sport of ultrarunning. However, the marathon holds a special place in my heart and is the race I wish everyone would attempt at least once. Running is not for everyone, and I do understand this distance may not be for every runner.

I'd be lying if I said, "It can't hurt to try." I've yet to run a painless marathon, but what would a challenge be without a little struggle? To run this distance just to cross a finish line may seem absurd, but I can assure you that we discover more about ourselves along the way than whether or not we're capable of finishing. As for me, it is more about the journey along the way than the time it took to get there. My reasoning and purpose for running as I do are sprinkled throughout this entire book. Not only do I have a lot to learn about running, I also have a lot to learn from running.

Running is symbolic to life in many ways. Some miles seem easy, while others are tough to get through. Life is challenging, but we emerge from the rubble of our obstacles stronger. It can break us down to a point where there isn't an ounce of strength left reserved. Mental and physical depletion leave us stranded without a drop of fight to spare. Those who have been there in life can agree. Ironically, this is what a marathon can bestow upon us: a breakdown of strength and will. It strips us down to nothing and reveals whatever happens to be left. This is partly what drives me to the marathon. The taste of despair and an all-too-familiar sense of what it feels like to be hit with a ton of bricks.

I like the taste of that feeling because it continues to expose who I am and what I'm made of. It is my way of fighting back and stepping up to the plate against something greater than myself. The marathon tries to convince me that I am destructible, yet every single time I emerge the exact opposite. This strengthens my character more and more with each attempt. This race has its history with me, as it's my story of David and Goliath. I've never come close to winning a marathon, but even more important to me is that I have never come close to losing the fight.

The Finisher Medal

If it were entirely up to me, the office in our home would be littered with finisher medals. I hang my favorite ten, and rotate the others in and out to add some flavor, color, and personality. This is by far one of the best icons within the running culture. The ribbon is artistically detailed or even customized with the date when the race was held. The medal itself is heavily weighted and features a design unique to each specific race. No finisher medal is the same, as each race has tailored the medal toward its own exclusive theme. The finisher medal is what's placed around ours neck when we cross the finish line.

A finisher medal symbolizes the hard work and dedication, all of our training, and the successful completion of another personal goal. Besides the ten selected medals hanging in my office, there are zippered bags full of them stashed away in my closet. Why are they stashed away in bags? My wife would never let me decorate all of the wall space with them. She throws her medals in a sock drawer, never to provide them the respect they deserve. One would think my wife was actually thoughtful by purchasing a rack to display my medals. However, this was just her attempt to set the parameters and minimize the actual wall space dedicated to hanging my most cherished items, my finisher medals.

Each one of these medals carries a memory. When I sort through my medals, I remember each race, and most likely the details of how it unfolded. I remember what the struggles were and what it took to get to the finish line. I even remember the strangers I met and ran with along the way. Never was there a race that was too easy, abandoning all effort out there on the race course. Each medal tells a story, as it took my blood, sweat, and tears to earn each accomplishment.

Have you heard a song playing recently that reminds you of childhood? Doesn't music take you to a specific time in your life, an entire train of thought packed with different emotions and feelings? These memories trigger other memories of times in our lives we didn't even know we remembered. This is why it isn't just a finisher medal to me but an artistic icon that jogs memories from the past. They tell an entire story and represent the challenge I've given myself. Finisher medals are personal to me because they prompt me to reminisce about the meaning of my journey and in ways I may not have ordinarily remembered.

Gifts of Healthy Running

Running offers immense benefits in an all-encompassing manner. Improving our own physical and mental health is not only beneficial in the present but could add years to our life and give those future years additional quality. It's an excellent means of conditioning our cardiovascular system, as running can simultaneously reduce our risk for developing heart disease. The reduction of blood pressure and even cholesterol begins to promote a healthier blood flow.

The bone density, which is important as we continue to age, tends to increase through weight-bearing activities such as running. Our bones adapt to the load they are placed under. Running causes new bone tissue formation, thus providing the density and strength that's necessary for our overall health. We undergo changes to body composition such as fat loss and muscle gain, and we also begin to increase our metabolic rate, the rate at which our bodies expend energy. Running has also shown to improve neurological function and reduces the risk of future cognitive decline such as Alzheimer's disease and other forms of dementia. The psychological component isn't excluded at all, as running releases endorphins, which decrease levels of stress, anxiety, and even depression. While running may not be for everyone, it's tough to argue with an enormous list of benefits like that.

Being a runner over the past ten years has required consistent dedication and sacrifice. I am eternally grateful for the health to currently run as much as I want to. Running a race is an emotional experience, not just when crossing the finish line but before I even start. It makes an impact on me when gratitude sets in that I am healthy enough to partake in such events. It's a blessing to test our limits further than our minds can dream, and discover that what we thought were our limitations may very well be a new beginning and the start to an entirely new journey.

PART 2:

Preliminary Training

"You must do the thing you think you cannot do."

—Eleanor Roosevelt

CHAPTER 4:

Goal Setting

Journey through Perceived Limitations

It is very important to have a vision in life, a constant visual of ever-changing purpose. Even more important is constructing a blueprint, the plan and direction for how to accomplish it. The vision and blueprint are but a fragment, however, for without the mental fortitude to make the decision and take that leap, the accomplishment remains a vision and fails to transpire. The path of our journey begins with setting a goal, the process of identifying what we want to accomplish and establishing measurable steps and time frames toward its achievement. Measurable goals, or steps, such as workout sessions, training runs, and even strategically placed races along the way are of main importance. These smaller and more feasible goals throughout the journey can keep us on track, provide a confidence boost, and help break the monotony of training for four to six months at a time. Develop a meaning and purpose as to why you have chosen the endeavor, because that should prove to be the motivating factor against the arduous peak you're attempting to climb.

Invariably, my goal selection consists of those that appear to be out of reach, particularly ones I'm skeptical about whether or not I can even attain. Although there is a small fraction of doubt, the most challenging journey becomes the most rewarding endeavor. This psychological ambition entertains the notion I can push the limit between real and perceived limitations. If reality is aligned with my current capabilities, the push beyond creates a unique opportunity to give reality the advancement it deserves. Forced out of my comfort zone, these moments offer me the chance to venture and navigate through unknown territory. This is where we unlock our true strength and hidden potential, and at levels that we don't ordinarily have access to.

My preference is setting goals that push my own limitations further, as opposed to attempting the outright impossible. I believe it is better to climb an incremental ladder of success one step at a time, rather than continuously fail trying to bypass multiple steps that should have been taken along the way. Testing my perceived limitations continues to prove that barriers can be surpassed and pushed further toward the distant horizons. Setting goals such as these gives me opportunities to demonstrate that I am capable of more than I could have ever imagined.

Fear: Inhibition or Motivation

To choose a goal that is considered slightly out of reach is voluntarily creating the perfect fraction of fear when attempting to exceed perceived limitations. How far out of reach is the question, because attempting the impossible redlines our fear gauge, which can then inhibit our initiative and drive to succeed. Choosing a goal within this particular spectrum is a sweet spot, because it offers enough chance to succeed and a smaller margin to fail. The perfect fraction of fear could stem from being afraid to dedicate so much time and energy and make so many sacrifices toward a goal I may not accomplish.

These are the types of goals to cherish, as they tend to offer additional motivating factors. If the accomplishment were absolutely certain, we wouldn't pour in all the blood, sweat, and tears; the challenge just wouldn't be worth that level of commitment. However, when there is just the right amount of doubt about our success and a sliver of failure remains an option, it may have the ability to motivate us beyond belief. This concept applies to running and any other goal, for that matter. It is about finding your spectrum of what is realistic and what is just out of reach and staying within that range.

Venturing into the realm of unrealistic goals could increase the probability of failure, and therefore discourage us from putting forth the effort and sacrifice necessary to succeed. This is not to say an unrealistic goal is impossible, but rather that it only increases the probability of failure and decreases the probability of success. On the opposite end of the spectrum, a goal that is completely within reach and obviously obtainable deprives us of the opportunity to advance to the next level. Settling for stagnation, which lacks growth and development, can make the completion of our goal rather ungratifying and anticlimactic.

I believe a healthy dose of fear is a motivator, as our physical performance and psychological mindset differ than when this emotion is nonexistent. I theorize that this healthy dose lies within the spectrum discussed above. On the other hand, too much fear can begin to inhibit even attempting to engage in what's necessary to actually succeed. Use fear as an indicator, and choose a goal you have always wanted to accomplish but always thought was impractical. Smaller goals that are within reach will place that ultimate goal just within your spectrum of reality.

Unrealistic and Impossible Goals

As our ambition intensifies, so will the complexity of converting our dreams into a reality. In this case, it may be that our ultimate goal requires longer periods of time to accomplish, more self-discipline and sacrifice, and an even greater amount of mental fortitude. But this does not necessarily mean it cannot be accomplished or that it's unrealistic or impossible. A hundred, or even a thousand, miniature realistic goals to hurdle in order to accomplish the impossible doesn't necessarily imply that the overall success of that goal is impossible.

The viewpoint and stance I take toward unthinkable or inconceivable events is by asking how we can make unrealistic goals reality, and how to make impossible goals a possibility. The time frame to accomplish this depends on the difference between current capability and the desired one. It could take six months or it could take three years. In either case, I'm fully convinced that by filling that time frame with realistic and achievable goals along the way, helps you to inch closer and closer toward the conclusive desire. The value in forecasting thought this far forward is the simple fact that time will pass whether we are striving for accomplishment or not. Those six months or three years will come to pass regardless of how we've chosen to invest our time and energy.

Your goal may be to start running or it may be to run a marathon. Perhaps it's to complete an ultramarathon or run across an entire state. Some people have run across the entire United States, a goal that is obviously within the realm of human potential. I do not want to assume something is unrealistic and impossible, and instead apply clever and creative ways to place it within arm's reach. It may require hurdling many barriers and a greater amount of time before the opportunity; however, that time will pass regardless of whether you've inched yourself closer or not. When the time comes, I can guarantee it will be pleasing to know it was spent accomplishing long-term goals that you assumed were unachievable. We build on top of what we've built, and this continuing year after year can begin to make unrealistic goals reality and impossible goals a possibility.

Challenges Compound over Time

Being goal oriented and having the drive and persistence to overcome the challenges we've placed in front of ourselves could be viewed no differently than a double-edged sword. On one hand, it is extremely gratifying to overcome something we thought we never could. On the other hand, it plants a seed and creates thoughts about whether something greater could have been accomplished. This creates the compounding effect of increasing drive and ambition. The succession of goal completion creates a snowball effect and, as the snowball plows onward, it continues to grow in size and speed. Gaining strength and stamina along the way, we have sufficient force and momentum to utilize in each race. But what if that ultimate race, the one we have been training for all along, is yet another short-term goal on a much larger scale? What if every year, our ultimate race is just another experience to assist us further along on our journey?

I used to think my main accomplishments were self-explanatory and that I would be content knowing they were possible to overcome. I'm finding, over time, that those main accomplishments were mere stepping-stones along the path of my journey and assist in the achievement of future endeavors. The reasoning for these ultimate goals is wide-ranging, and tends to demonstrate evidence of additional opportunity beyond what was originally anticipated. So, the question may become why do I continue down this road, a path where ultimate goals are then perceived as mere stepping-stones?

I am in the process of paving my way to create a unique and personal journey into the unknown, and the only way to do so is to bring new stepping-stones into existence. With each new placement of stone, it extends my spectrum of reality, and what was out of reach becomes just within reach. Once another stone is placed, reality extends further and opportunity seeps closer. What appears to be a mile away begins to inch its way closer over time with each accomplishment. Though it may only continue to expose evidence of additional opportunity beyond what was originally anticipated, it is exactly why my ultimate goals and the reasoning for them are wide-ranging.

This seems to be the only way I can describe what it feels like to be primed and loaded with meaning and purpose. And though some assume I am chasing something without end, it only reinforces my argument there may not be an end. My meaning and purpose involve the pursuit of endless possibility; therefore, it stands to reason this is an infinite construction of preliminary groundwork. This vision, the blueprint and direction of my meaning and purpose, grows more evident toward my seeking out endless possibility.

The time we invest in our preparation, and the training we have committed to endure, will be exactly what slings us past our perceived limitations. If we are to extend our pathway, even if it is only to catch a glimpse of our next opportunity, we must do so in such a way that solidifies a foundation of stable groundwork. As we begin to reinforce our physical and mental strength, the emphasis remains on building an impenetrable mind, as this becomes the only way I've overcome challenges that compound over time.

CHAPTER 5:

The Preparation

The Investment to Prepare

There is a variety of descriptive meanings associated with the word training, but among them all preparation paints the picture best. Preparation is the action of making ourselves ready for an event or undertaking. The key word is undertaking, which means a formal pledge or promise to follow through with our goal. This pledge is to ourselves, and is the easiest to make, yet sometimes the toughest to fulfill. Losing sight of our goals could mean we failed to prepare for the training itself. If we understand fully what preparation is and what an undertaking means, then we are ready to walk the path toward the journey we've laid out in front of ourselves.

There are many important steps before even beginning the physical workouts and training sessions. Sometimes it seems like diving right into the physical training is an impulsive, but understandable means to initiate the training process. However, it begins with premeditative preparation, such as goal-setting, making the commitment and pledge to ourselves we will follow through, and an understanding that the training process means complete devotion toward a substantial investment.

Training is simply a means of investing our time and energy into what will yield the best possibilities for success. We trade our time and energy through sacrifice, in order to become physically and mentally capable of attempting the challenge we've placed upon ourselves. The conditions we endure through training and how much we commit to are indicative of the likelihood we will succeed and achieve our goal. When it comes to our training, the question is not how busy we are but how much of a priority our goal has become.

Cherish the training process, as each workout session is like a nominal deposit in a bank account. Depositing even the smallest amounts consistently over a large period of time means the balance grows to become something extraordinary. This bank account, however, is no ordinary savings account but one that accrues interest and compounds over time. Benefits don't come without the price of our efforts, because to be diligently prepared for success and accomplishment takes immense sacrifice, self-discipline, and consistency. Though all are equally important, the lack of consistency tends to be what drives people away from their goals and ambitions. So, allow me to reiterate: Training takes consistency of self-discipline and sacrifice. It is vital to perform the training necessary over a large span of time and, perhaps more importantly, in a consistent manner.

A training plan should be carefully thought out, and must be considered honestly. A training plan that is too aggressive will surely mean unnecessary pressure and frustration, increase the likelihood of falling short, and place us at risk for injury. A plan that is too conservative for our experience may not place on us the demands necessary to excel and grow as a runner. There are so many training plans available online that it is hard to imagine I need to include any in this book. A runner has different options when choosing a training plan: researching the plethora of those available on the internet and tweaking one if necessary, hiring a running coach to guide them through the process, or, if experienced enough, creating one themselves. I have developed a passion for creating my own training plans as I continue to grow and evolve as a runner. Different goals and new capabilities call for a unique and creative approach toward development.

Creating or searching for a plan within or just outside our capabilities is where honesty enters the equation. I have surely bitten off more than I can chew, but perhaps that's a feeling training is supposed to instill. If we are preparing ourselves for something we've never done before and wish to succeed, it makes sense for us to find or create a training plan just outside of our current potential. On the other hand, it's important not to sabotage ourselves from the beginning by selecting or creating a plan we may not realistically and consistently stick to. Training plans are tools, templates created to get us where we want to go. Each person responds to training differently and a training plan is never uniformly applicable to every runner. The simple message is to find out what works for you, which can be found through experience, experimentation, or even the guidance of a coach or mentor.

How do we stay dedicated for such timeframes? Does the motivation fade or waver over time? Training is meant to be uncomfortable, as it wouldn't take us to the next level if it weren't. Each individual is different, and so must find ways to avoid the distractions that keep us from being laser focused and goal oriented. This is not an easy process, as training will not reveal the results we expect at the moments we demand. It is a gradual process that builds toward the peak we're slowly ascending, and we must exercise patience along the way. This entire process is only a mindset, one we must set in place from the very beginning. Keeping this mindset steady and learning how to turn it on when we need it most can be the difference between victory and falling short.

Training Is a Mindset

The alarm sounds at four o'clock in the morning. It's raining outside and I have a long day ahead of me. I haven't slept much at all, as parenting duties call throughout the night regardless of circumstance. I have been training for months and I feel like I haven't had a break. Between my full-time job, parenting, traveling, and the training I've committed myself to, it wouldn't be hard to fall back asleep and catch up on my rest. Besides, it's raining and extremely dark, and I have planned to run twelve miles of Old Cutler Trail before my workday even begins. *That trail will be there tomorrow, won't it?*

Self-talk can be very persuasive at times, should we choose to listen. Metaphorically speaking, it knows precisely where to aim its blade and even when to strike. These are the times our mind will not motivate us and will actually strip away our incentives if we give it permission to. The physical benefits of training are only by-products of successful mental training, because without the mental fortitude to dismiss the reasoning to quit, we will never see an inkling of physical benefit. The scenario described above isn't fictional, as it was a common occurrence during my training for the Cross Florida 116. These are perhaps the most valuable mental training opportunities that arise, for they not only sharpen our ability to quiet the mind but help us realize that overcoming the excuse to quit is far better than accepting it.

Do we want to rise victorious or taste the possibility of failure? The mind will ask us this from many different angles and disguise itself from the question above. The mind does not hesitate to strike when we're weak, as that's when we're most likely to cave in to its masterful trickery. Ironically, we use the same mind when fighting the urge to quit as we do when we falter and decide to give in. So, which mindset do we want to strengthen, the urge to fight or the urge to quit? This is the essence of mental training.

The intuition to do the opposite of what our mind may advise may not always be apparent, obvious, or even glaring. In fact, the justifications and excuses to quit may continue to strengthen if that is what we choose to empower. Without this ability to act upon the contrary, negate its trickery, and stay true to our goals and ambitions regardless of circumstance, we fall victim to the failure of not following through with our pledge and commitment. From the preparation phase, all the way through training and until we reach the finish line of whatever goal we choose to pursue, this unfaltering mindset is required from beginning to end. These are the most valuable opportunities and lessons in training, and failure to see these as such will decrease the odds of successful training. If we neglect opportunities for successful mental training, the physical aspect of training becomes obsolete. Remember, our journey begins by seeking to transform what is impossible into the beginning of possibility, but that transformation will not occur without the consistency of immense sacrifice from a self-disciplined mindset.

PART 3:

The Application of Training

"Courage is not having the strength to go on; it is going on when you don't have the strength."

-Theodore Roosevelt

CHAPTER 6:

Guidelines and Principles

Frequency, Intensity, and Duration

Frequency, intensity, and duration are perhaps the most important concepts of physical training and will be the cornerstone of decision-making throughout the training process. The understanding or insight into each of these segments can increase overall safety and reduce the risk of injury. When an injury or setback occurs, it is most likely due to an ongoing increase in frequency, intensity, and duration before the body is ready to absorb the stress. Training is a gradual process, as the body requires time to recover and prepare from the stress loads that are applied. The impact placed on the body can be monitored and balanced through the manipulation of frequency, intensity, and duration.

Frequency is simply how often training occurs, or the number of times you run in any given week. Running four times in a given week is a frequency of four runs that week. Frequency doesn't care about distance covered or the specific pace run. Nailing down an initial and consistent frequency on a per-week basis to build upon is, perhaps, one of the most important places to begin in training. Having a solid base of frequency prior to the initial week of training can strategically position the mind and body for success throughout the entire training schedule.

Intensity is specifically about the effort exerted and the speed run, which can be measured several different ways including pace, heart rate, or rating of perceived exertion. Most runners track pace and/or heart rate to modify or manipulate workout intensity. The higher the intensity level, the quicker exhaustion will present itself. Workouts can include sprints, track repeats, tempo runs, and *fartlek* running (Swedish for speed play). All show an uptick of intensity levels when compared to an aerobic lower-intensity base pace (70 to 80 percent of maximum heart rate, roughly calculated by subtracting age from 220). Sessions that focus on intensity develop anaerobic strength (80 to 90 percent of maximum heart rate), for efficiency, speed, and power. Intensity requires gradual adaptation and thus should also be increased incrementally.

The duration of a run is measured by time and/or distance. How much time was spent running, or how long a distance was covered? This too should be incrementally progressed, as pushing the limits weekly in each of these three categories only opens the door for risk of overuse. Increasing intensity will automatically decrease the duration, as intensity and duration are inversely proportionate. This is simply because the more effort exerted into the run, the quicker exhaustion will occur. However, the additional stress that increased intensity places on the body will more than make up for any decrease of duration.

There are two additional points to take into consideration. The more frequently we run, the less time is available for recovery. Likewise, the higher the intensity levels of running, the more time required for the body to recover. Taking this into consideration could help us achieve the appropriate balance for training progression. Risk factors increase drastically when a runner decides to build frequency, intensity, and duration all within the same week, and perhaps continues this behavior over subsequent weeks. Injuries may not always present themselves immediately, but may arrive a week or two after from the decisions made over previous weeks.

Focus on the varying combinations of these three categories should depend on goals and timelines. Some runners, like me, gravitate more toward long-distance training and may shift focus toward frequency and duration. Others tend to find joy in speed work or shorter-distance races, and may place more emphasis on frequency and intensity. Every runner should assess their own goals and timelines and determine a training plan suitable to meet their needs. The importance of a timeline depends on the fitness level when training begins.

The concepts surrounding frequency, intensity, and duration do not discriminate against a runner's experience level, as each runner has their own line to walk and tipping points to avoid. There aren't many ways to gain experience without the time spent experimenting, but tampering with the maximum line of tolerance only increases risk and is not necessarily worth the benefits or additional cardiovascular strengthening. When in doubt, err on the side of caution; the benefits don't outweigh the consequences. Our decision-making with regard to frequency, intensity, and duration has everything to do with our success and safety as a runner.

The 10 Percent Rule

A common rule or advisable guideline to follow during training is known as the 10 percent rule. This generally means not to exceed, or to utilize caution when, increasing weekly mileage more than 10 percent the following week. For instance, running a twenty-mile week should allow a safe increase up to approximately twenty-two miles the following week. Likewise, running a sixty-mile week means the body is prepared to handle an approximate sixty-six miles. This is how ramping up weekly mileage happens at a gradual and steady rate. This is also why it takes time to build up to high-volume training weeks, especially when including a reduction of mileage every fourth week to allow the body time to recover.

When increasing mileage three weeks in a row, the fourth week should taper the overall mileage approximately 20 to 30 percent. This scaling back allows the body to recover, as well as providing a beneficial mental and physical reprieve. A month-long training period can be viewed as three steps forward and one step backward. Following a three-week progression, the recovery week gives the body time to heal and repair itself before increasing the stress load and resuming the training progression once again.

The 10 percent guideline may not need to be as stern during low-mileage and low-intensity levels, but may require more adherence as training volume and/or intensity increase. Running low mileage at low intensity levels tends to have more wiggle room concerning this rule, and could probably be stretched more so than when training at very high-intensity levels or high-volume mileage. Through experience and experimentation, I've found I can increase more than 10 percent per week up to a certain point, until I arrive at the level of training where I respect and adhere to the 10 percent rule. While each runner is unique and has different levels of experience with training, everyone has a point where they must scale back and adhere to certain guidelines.

I am definitely one to test limits, push boundaries, and seek endless possibility. I also understand the necessity to arrive at my destination safely. My first destination is the starting line of the race I am training for. A healthy start means a fair shot at the challenge I'm seeking to accomplish. It's easy to jump ahead and only visualize crossing the finish line, but failing to understand the importance of a safe and healthy arrival to the start means there won't be a fair shot at finishing. While I urge everyone to test limits and push boundaries of what is possible, we all have a tipping point that can compromise the opportunity entirely. Train hard, but train smart. Utilize the frequency, intensity, and duration concepts along with the 10 percent rule where you must. Training is about experimentation and discovering what works for you and what doesn't. When you find yourself in doubt, remember the risk may not necessarily outweigh the reward.

Principle of Specificity

Specific adaption to imposed demands (SAID principle) is the framework of specificity, a necessary foundation on which training programs shall be constructed. Simply put, the training performed should be relevant and appropriate for the desired result or necessary outcome. If we want to be better distance runners, we have to run longer distances. To be a faster runner, we have to run at a faster pace. Specificity means we will have to repetitiously perform the skill we want to excel at. It sounds obvious, but some athletes may invest too much into non-specific training that may not maximize their overall results. I utilize this principle to give each workout meaning and purpose. What is the reasoning for each workout, and can it provide the desired result or necessary outcome?

Specificity of training refers to the specific type of running that is performed towards more specific goals. Training methods must be used that move toward the desired adaptation. Shorter distances with faster time goals require more speed work and tempo running as opposed to a runner attempting an ultra-marathon, which involves a higher volume of weekly mileage. The type of running performed facilitates the recruitment of different muscle fibers, which maximizes training and yields the best return on the investment of time and energy. Specificity of training provides the highest chances of success to meet the demands our goals require.

When my training deviates from running, I attempt to remain as specific as possible. In this regard, it is relevant to acknowledge a transfer of training, or the overflow of benefit, that can be brought about through cross-training. Choosing to invest a fraction of time in cross-training introduces benefits such as injury prevention, addressing muscle imbalance through active recovery, and a psychological change when running becomes monotonous. By seeking muscle balance, the risk for injury is equalized by incorporating complimentary activities that address these concerns. Cross-training can be incorporated as an insurance policy while keeping specificity at the forefront of the mind.

CHAPTER 7:

Finding Muscle Balance

Cross-Training

Cross-training, or the overflow effect, is the belief that performing non-specific activity will benefit the performance and sport of choice. Cross-training is engaging in two or more types of exercise to improve performance in a primary sport. Many positive factors arise from engaging in cross-training, such as injury prevention, balancing of muscle length and strength, and a psychological reprieve from the monotony of running. When cross-training is integrated into my weekly regimen, I carefully select the activity for how it can benefit my regular workout. In other words, I expect it to have a certain result and effect on my running, as this is what I am choosing to invest my precious time and energy into as the substitute for a run. There can be times in training when a non-specific activity can be more beneficial than an additional weekly run.

What sport or activity should be considered? My selection depends on whether it meets the criteria of injury prevention, rebalancing muscle length and strength, and providing a psychological rejuvenation. Why, or the understanding of how a non-specific activity meets these criteria, is important, and that comprehension only increase its necessity and inclusion. Where it fits into the training schedule is the other question to consider. Its strategic placement is crucial, as we want to maximize its effect and only substitute the training runs that can technically be afforded. Addressing the what, why, and where questions can help determine the selection of the most specific secondary activity or sport to compliment running.

I offer three examples of cross-training activities that could be utilized in order to reduce the overall impact of running while increasing or maintaining cardiovascular strength. All three address the endurance aspect of training specific to running, which implies that the results can be transferrable. Furthermore, they can begin to engage bodily musculature in various ways that running doesn't, ultimately working all of the same muscle groups in several different ways. The additional benefit of these options is they are low or non-impact and weight or non-weight bearing activities, offering active recovery in the middle or toward the end of a long training week. The reasoning and selection for each activity can be extended in multiple directions, because it depends on your goals, benefits, and current situation throughout training. The what, why, and where questions can help steer you in the right direction, while keeping in mind that these are merely three examples out of a plethora of options.

Cycling is a weight-bearing, low-impact sport and offers tremendous benefit and transferrable results toward running. Aside from the endurance and cardiovascular component, the modification of resistance begins to increase the overall hip and knee muscular strength in varying ways. The muscles used, which act as the primary source of force that propel a runner forward, differ slightly than those used during cycling. Promoting gluteal and quadriceps/hamstrings development, the hips and knees are provided the strength and stability necessary to combat against the ground reaction forces encountered while running. This can begin the process of muscle rebalancing by utilizing the same muscle groups in many different ways, which can negate the overuse and repetitive nature brought upon by repeated running.

Swimming is a non-weight bearing and non-impact sport that also targets the cardiovascular aspect of endurance training and has transferrable results. Unique to swimming is the possibility of being able to maintain fitness levels if an injury or setback is experienced due to the elimination of the impact and weight-bearing components of other kinds of activity. Water can be a fascinating use of resistance and provides an upper-body workout that can't be replicated with running. Swimming can be a great way to rid or shake out lower-body soreness that may be lingering from previous hard workouts. Needless to say, it can also offer a great psychological reprieve should running become monotonous or too repetitive.

An elliptical machine is a weight-bearing and low-impact activity. Through resistance modification, the machine can offer not only the endurance of cardiovascular strengthening but also the incorporation of the arms, shoulders, chest, back, and core musculature in ways running may not. The elliptical mimics some upper-body benefits from swimming, as well as the same weight-bearing, low-impact effects of cycling. Additional benefits to using an elliptical are the ability to pedal forward and backward, each of which engages each muscle group differently. As mentioned earlier, it completely depends on each individual's goals, current situation, and the targeted benefits desired.

My suggestion to achieve maximum results from the time and energy invested into cross-training is to address each of these dynamics: provide reasoning for why it is specific to running and how it is transferrable, and provide reasoning for how it can meet the criteria of injury prevention, muscle balancing, and a psychological reprieve. Activities and sports such as these can be hybrid in nature, as they provide not only cardiovascular endurance but muscle strengthening in a multitude of ways. As we begin to venture into strengthening and stretching, they, too, can be employed for very specific reasons. This begins to place more emphasis on injury prevention and an even greater emphasis on muscular balance.

Strengthening

My view on strength training differs from those who prioritize it completely. Strength training compliments my running and is incorporated for two reasons:

1. to enhance muscle performance
2. to act as a countermeasure against risk for injury

Strength training addresses three key elements of muscle performance:

1. strength

2. speed

3. endurance

Increasing strength is highly transferrable to the sport of running, regardless of whether your goals entail speed or running long distances. Having a basic understanding and awareness of how to challenge muscle can provide greater benefits and maximize our results to an even greater extent.

The *overload principle* states that in order for muscle performance to improve, we must place a load upon it that exceeds the capacity of that muscle. It is the guiding principle of exercise and the foundation of how and why muscle performance is improved. Muscle must be challenged for it to perform to a greater degree. Likewise, if the demand remains constant at what the muscle has adapted to, performance maintenance is all to be expected. Depending on the variance in overall goals from one runner to the next, it can make a difference how each individual engages in strength training.

Muscle performance is how efficiently the capacity of a muscle generates force. The three key elements of strength, power, and endurance contribute to the muscles' performance and can be targeted specifically depending on goals. The muscle's *strength* is the greatest measurable force that can be exerted by a muscle or muscle group to overcome resistance. Muscle *power* relates to the strength and speed of a movement. In other words, the work produced by the muscle within a specific time or distance. Muscle *endurance* is the ability to perform a low-intensity repetitive activity over a sustained period of time. Endurance is the muscle's ability to repetitively contract against a load or resistance and simultaneously resist that fatigue for an extended period of time.

Are your goals to become more swift and agile or is it to build endurance to complete long-distance challenges? Modification of resistance and number of repetitions can involve either fast- or slow-twitch muscle fibers, which are tailored to the success with either speed or long-distance running respectively. Fast-twitch muscle fibers drive explosive power, for quick and powerful movements, that can be recruited through low-repetition/heavy-resistance weight training. On the contrary, slow-twitch muscle fibers for muscle-endurance training can be facilitated through high repetitions of light resistance. For example, performing five sets of five repetitions utilizing heavy weight begins to recruit fast-twitch muscle fibers, which can translate to strength and power, whereas performing three sets of thirty repetitions against light resistance recruits slow-twitch muscle fibers, translating to the muscle-fatigue resistance required for stamina and endurance training.

Runners who wish to enhance speed can focus on strength and power, with focus on heavy weight and explosive movement; those who emphasize long-distance running can focus on strength and endurance through light weight and high repetitions. While it can be beneficial to integrate all three key elements of muscle performance, this is simply a means of customizing your training according to time availability, degree of belief in the principle of specificity, and the actual results produced from the application of these methods. The achievement of a solid foundation of muscle performance could signify the appropriate time to customize the ratio of varying muscle fiber recruitment. Bear in mind that some runners are genetically predisposed to a different muscle-fiber ratio when compared to other runners, so further recruitment of muscle fiber types can be easier or more difficult depending on the genetic cards that were dealt.

Functional fitness exercises train muscles to work together and can also be classified as compound-movement exercises. These exercises work more than one muscle and at more than one joint simultaneously. Examples are push-ups, sit-ups, pull-ups, squats, lunges, and so on. Incorporating muscles of the upper and lower body concurrently integrates the all-important core musculature. Isolation exercises target one specific muscle and will usually incorporate movement at one particular joint. Again, while it is beneficial to train numerous muscle groups to work together (muscle synergy), it can be as important to isolate one muscle or muscle group at a time to customize the achievement of muscle balance. The mixture of compound and isolation exercises will continue to challenge muscle and remove the predictability of repetitious workouts a muscle or muscle group may have adapted to. Forcing muscle to adapt to change will enhance the muscle's performance as opposed to simply maintaining it.

When transitioning from strengthening skeletal muscle (muscle that connects to bone and provides skeletal movement) to strengthening cardiac muscle, it is important to recognize obvious similarities and differences. The heart is made up of cardiac muscle tissue and, thus, can be challenged and strengthened similarly through aerobic and anaerobic activities (cardio). Contrary to how the skeletal muscles contract through voluntary movement, the heart pumps oxygenated blood without a conscious decision. How can the cardiac muscle be challenged voluntarily if its contractions are involuntary? The same concepts of strengthening, ironically, apply, and it is noteworthy to touch upon and elaborate on the topic.

The greater the intensity of running, the faster the heart will contract to pump oxygenated blood to the working muscles. This occurs in an attempt to keep pace with the workout's demand. Running at a pace greater than can be sustained creates an increasing respiratory rate and hyperventilation. The performing skeletal muscles demand the majority of oxygenated blood, which is why runners at high intensity gasp for air trying to maintain an unsustainable pace. Welcome to the anaerobic state (80 to 90 percent effort), which creates oxygen debt; lactate accumulation in the muscles, leading to overall fatigue; and a cessation of the workout if the pace isn't decreased. Anaerobic strengthening is obviously catered toward runners who wish to become faster, which over time will lead to the sustainability of a faster pace for a longer period of time. But how can this faster pace be sustained for a longer duration of time?

Aerobic training is the foundation of the ability to maintain a specific pace for increasing periods and duration of time. Without aerobic strength, the distance will eventually halt us in our tracks. Aerobic strengthening is being performed when running in lower heart-rate zones and is primarily due to its lower overall levels of intensity. Without tracking heart rate, you can assume you're in an aerobic state when running if you are able to hold a conversation with someone. If an increased respiratory rate is interrupting your sentence or conversation, you are beginning to enter an anaerobic state. This is why the aerobic state is also termed a conversational pace. This is running that does not create oxygen debt or make the runner hyperventilate, because it is a pace that is sustainable for longer periods of time. As aerobic capacity strengthens over time, the heart's oxygen-delivering capability leads to a greater degree of cardiac efficiency. The evidence is apparent when running a faster pace with a seemingly equivalent effort as the previously slower pace. A decrease of resting heart rate over time is strictly due to the improving cardiac efficiency, such as the performance of the same tasks with less perceived exertion. This is how a faster pace or even-further distances are run, and we become more efficient, economic runners.

In summary, we begin to enhance skeletal muscle performance through the use of strength training. Once that framework is built, the ratio between the recruitment of fast- and slow-twitch muscle fibers can be modified, targeting either power or endurance training. By incorporating functional or compound exercises to enhance muscle synergy and isolating muscles to customize balance, we begin to address our own particular needs for our own specific goals. When coupling strength training for skeletal muscles, and the aerobic/anaerobic demands on our cardiovascular systems, we can begin to create an extremely resilient and efficient, well-balanced runner. Strengthening to any degree should be incorporated if your desire is to: run faster and/or further, to address the three key elements of muscle performance, or wish to achieve muscle balance as a countermeasure against the risk of injury.

Stretching

Many questions and debates surround the topic of stretching, primarily because it's subjective and differs from runner to runner. *Should I stretch? If so, should I stretch before or after running? Which is more preferable, static or dynamic stretching? What is the difference between active and passive stretching?* These are areas where having basic insight could help an individual derive the best possible solutions for themselves, and this is yet another category where my answers or beliefs may differ from yours.

Now, whether a runner should stretch, which muscles, and to what degree is a whole other topic. Some runners are naturally hypermobile (a greater joint range of motion), while others have hypomobility (decreased joint range of motion). I have always been hypermobile, a very flexible person who naturally has a greater range of motion at each joint than the average individual. On the other hand, I know people that are so hypomobile they require immense stretching to even come close to the joint range I have always possessed. So, to make a general statement that everyone should stretch would be entirely erroneous.

Running basically requires hundreds or even thousands of muscle contractions depending on the distance the body covers. During each concentric muscle contraction, there is a shortening of muscle length and an increase of muscle tension, which changes the angle of the joints and produces movement. Over time, as training progresses, the force-producing muscle fibers become shorter and retain more tension. Generally, this can bring about feelings of muscle tightness and joint stiffness. Without intervention, this process can eventually begin to affect the freedom of the joint's movement (range of motion). If the joint range or freedom becomes affected to any degree, the biomechanics become altered to a similar point and increase risk for injury. This contributes to the overuse of surrounding muscle groups and joint structures through compensatory strategies that often go unnoticed.

If a muscle repetitively contracts, as is the case during running, there must be an intervention somewhere along the line to negate the muscle-shortening process. Stretching the muscle in a sense lengthens it and releases that tension. Stretching is two-fold, as it not only begins to counter that shortened state of the muscle but decreases the tension that tends to accrue over time. In decreasing that tension, the muscle can begin to relax and start to lengthen. Picture a fist shut as tightly as possible; there is a lot of tension as all muscles involved are contracted. When it begins to relax, the tension eases and the muscles lengthen to release their grip.

The length-tension relationship of muscles is important to maintain, as lengthened or shortened muscle tends to have a minimal force production when compared to a muscle of balanced length and strength. For example, running has the tendency to shorten the hamstrings (a main force producer), and, as a result the quadriceps (a main stabilizer) become lengthened. The hamstrings are now contracting from a shortened state and the quadriceps are contracting from this lengthened state, causing a tendency to produce less force than if they initially contracted from their respective, optimal lengths. This impedes on overall efficiency and requires not only excess energy to compensate for less force production, but begins to increase risk of injury incrementally if the process continues without intervention.

By isolating and strengthening the quadriceps through knee extension, and stretching the hamstrings through hip flexion/knee extension, this muscular imbalance begins to reverse. This begins to shorten the quadriceps through strengthening and lengthens the hamstrings by stretching, which negates the imbalance created from running and begins moving the muscle groups toward ideal balance. While it may be unnecessary to comprehend these concepts, simply being introduced to the reasoning behind why a stretch is introduced can be of value depending on an individual's current circumstance.

The difference between active and passive stretching is simply whether you are stretching on your own (active), or whether someone else is doing the stretching for you (passive). Active stretching is when a muscle is lengthened, therefore placing a joint in a desired position and the stretch is maintained without the assistance of an external force. Performing an active stretch involves utilizing the strength of your own muscles to hold that position. On the other hand, passive stretching requires an external force to place and hold a muscle at a specific length, or a joint at a specified angle. Beneficially speaking, all bodily muscles can relax when being passively stretched, whereas active stretching involves the body's muscular engagement to hold a position. When thinking in terms of convenience, active stretching is always available, due to the simple fact it only requires ourselves and doesn't rely on external forces.

The differentiation between static and dynamic stretching is whether or not movement is incorporated. To keep it simple, a static stretch is when a muscle is placed in a lengthened position and held for a certain duration of time. Dynamic stretching is taking a muscle or muscle group through its desired length and joint range using repetitive movements, usually replicating the sport you're about to engage in. During a static stretch, the time frame and position held may vary depending on the intensity of the stretch. The greater the intensity of that stretch, the shorter duration of time it can be tolerated. The intensity depends on how much length the muscle is being taken through. I personally aim for a comfortable stretch until the tissue becomes pliable, which is when it can tolerate greater length and intensity.

Dynamic stretching is movement based, and can be utilized as a warm-up routine before high-intensity workouts. High-intensity workouts require the most available joint range and muscle elasticity, so warming up to that range before placing that particular demand on the body is highly advisable. Taking the time to perform a dynamic warm-up prior to an intense workout session could possibly prevent a muscle pull (strain), as breaking a sweat prior to the workout is one indicator that the muscles and tendons are in a more pliable state. While some runners perform a dynamic stretching program or warm-up routine, others may go for a light jog until perspiration (breaking a sweat) occurs. This particular topic is subjective, but through experience and experimentation you can begin to determine what works for you.

I'm often asked if I stretch, and my answers vary greatly depending on my current situation throughout my training program. If I am to perform a high-intensity workout, then I incorporate a dynamic warm-up routine and/ or run a slow-paced mile to warm up before starting the workout. However, if the workout is an easy run at an easy pace, there is no need for me to warm up; the entire run that day is at no greater intensity than my warm-up pace would be to begin with. As for whether I engage in static stretching, it, too, varies depending on my current circumstances. As I progress further into training, I begin allocating more time toward static stretching, mainly once I begin to feel muscle tightness occurring. Like most people, my daily schedule is busy and hectic, so I fit stretching in where I can and at the times that happen to be the most convenient. To make a long story short, I only stretch the muscles I need to, when I need to, and only to the degree I feel is required.

Stretching can be a wholesome means of lengthening the muscle to achieve its balance and to mitigate the risk for injury or setback. The incorporation of stretching won't completely prevent injury, as there are too many contributing factors that tend to cause it. However, I'm willing to bet there is a small percentage of runners who don't need to stretch at least some muscles, to some degree, during at least some point of their training duration. I've yet to hear about a running injury sustained by stretching, yet all too commonly injury occurs from overuse that could have stemmed from a muscular imbalance, and perhaps corrected through even a minimal routine of strengthening and stretching.

CHAPTER 8:

Injury Prevention

Proactive and Preventive Measures

Over the course of the past decade, I have come to understand the fact that injury prevention is simply part of my training and not a completely separate entity. While I place emphasis on the mental and physical aspects of training, it is equally important to include the safety components of injury prevention and recovery. I hope to clarify how we can drastically decrease our risk for setbacks or injury by focusing on two areas that are within our control: addressing muscle imbalance and avoiding overuse. I take a proactive stance to address muscle imbalance and a preventive stance to avoid overuse. This combination creates my recipe for success and longevity of running, injury free, and can help ensure a safe and healthy arrival at the starting line of our ultimate goal.

Muscular imbalances can be a contributing factor toward injury if not addressed through strengthening and stretching. Take a proactive approach to eliminate factors that can jeopardize further training or the ultimate goal itself. For example, those who may hold a sitting position for prolonged periods of time at work, at home, and driving are probably at risk for certain muscle imbalances that others may not be. Prolonged sitting throughout each day can cause muscle shortening and tightness of the iliopsoas (hip flexor) and hamstring musculature (knee flexors/hip extensors). This additionally creates a weakening of the quadriceps and gluteal musculature, very important hip and knee muscle groups, which require the proper firing and timing of muscle contractions when running.

Coincidently, running itself tends to increase the tension of the iliopsoas and hamstrings muscle group. Both prolonged sitting and running shortens the same muscle groups, so if the quadriceps and gluteal musculature is in a weakened state from a lack of strengthening, this will inevitably cause a problem area at some point along the hip, knee, and ankle kinetic chain. The stretching of the iliopsoas and hamstrings musculature (force producers), coupled with the strengthening of the quadriceps/gluteal muscle groups (main stabilizers), will restore balance and provide the safety and stabilization necessary to drastically reduce risk for injury.

Overuse injuries tend to crop up during irregular or improper training, such as increasing frequency, intensity, and duration prematurely or precipitously. The ground reaction forces placed upon the body during training can accumulate over time, and when the body is not given adequate time to recover through rest and recovery, it can eventually lead to issues down the road. Proper training balance each week, plus appropriate training progression each month can help prevent overuse scenarios from occurring. One aspect that could have an effect on our running economy and thus increase the risk for injury are biomechanical irregularities. While biomechanical irregularities, such as under or over pronation, can be partially corrected through use of proper footwear and gait analysis, other underlying factors are, to a certain degree, out of our control. So long as we are focusing on the areas within our control by addressing individualized muscle imbalances and attempting to avoid overuse scenarios, it can possibly offset the risk that irregular biomechanics might impose.

Each runner is unique in their own sort of way, ranging from differences in height and weight, joint alignments, patterns of foot strike, all the way to muscular synergies and skeletal structure. It would be next to impossible to find a perfectly symmetrical runner, as it's common to have at least some minor structural irregularity. Skeletal or structural symmetries within the body are more common than we think, and even the slightest ones affect our biomechanics when running. Again, focusing on the areas within our control, as in achieving muscular balance and avoiding overuse, may be enough to offset the possible risk that skeletal asymmetries out of our control may impose.

As a runner and throughout training, you will get to know yourself and your own body more than you ever have before. I've developed a system that works for me according to my own body's needs and potential problematic areas. Rather than allowing them to become an issue, I simply allocate some of my time and energy toward these needs throughout training, which has shown a tendency to prevent injury. I have developed my own recipe, yet it requires occasional tweaking as I progress through training and grow as a runner. Rather than having to completely halt training to treat injury, being proactive and taking preventive measures throughout training can contribute to success as we become safer, stronger, and more efficient runners.

Rest and Recovery

Many people misunderstand the irony of building strength during rest, and the weakening process that takes place during the act of training. The body rebuilds during recovery from the bodily breakdown caused during training. During workouts, we are actually in the process of breaking down the muscle tissue that was repaired during the previous rest day. The reason we endure more taxing and vigorous workouts through the gradual progression of training is because the body repairs itself to withstand not only the stress we've previously imposed but, as an additional margin of safety, a slightly greater demand. Neglecting rest and recovery can hinder the repair of our bodily tissue, which minimizes the effect of our workouts when our goal is to maximize training results. If we are placing strenuous effort into bodily breakdown, we must allocate time for bodily repair through a duration of rest and recovery.

This is precisely the reason I adhere to increasing weekly mileage by approximately 10 percent at a certain point in training, because that seems to be the additional mileage the body has repaired itself to safely withstand. So, if we get stronger when we rest and weaker when we train, which is technically of greater importance? It can be hard to gauge exactly how much rest is necessary to maximize results and fully absorb the demand we place on our bodies. Too much rest and we may not be training to full potential, while not enough rest may minimize the results from excess training. Training and recovery are both equal and essential components, which tend to complement one another as equivalents. We must find balance between the bodily breakdown and the rest and recovery counteraction to magnify the results of training and the time that we have sacrificed.

Feeling sluggish and fatigued during successive workout sessions is a beginning sign of over-training, and that the rest/recovery aspect of training may not be getting the attention it deserves. Scaling back on training to provide the body with additional rest can be more beneficial at times than engaging in another workout. Scheduling an extra day off to rest can be a necessary factor, as the miles lost can be redistributed over the following days or tossed altogether. There is no indicator that we can physically see, but it is something we begin to feel. Our bodies have ways of letting us know what may be too much or too little, and though it may not express itself immediately, it's important to listen when it does.

An additional way of incorporating recovery into training is the distribution of workouts over the course of the week. Alternating hard and easy workouts can balance the stress we are applying on the body, so as to not absorb the majority of the load within a fraction of that week. Interchanging the intensity or longer-distance running days with lower-intensity and-low mileage days can provide the opportunity for the bodily repair to help keep pace with the overall demand. Cramming intensity and distance into the beginning or end of the week does not provide ample time for rest and recovery, and may only increase the risk for a setback. Should life events dictate most workouts at the beginning or end of a week due to unusual circumstances, it is possible to safely rearrange workouts, and be sure to bookend that heavy portion of the week with rest and recovery.

The tapering of mileage every fourth week can be viewed as the recovery week, and should be taken seriously for obvious reasons. It is an opportunity for the physiology to repair itself from the previous three weeks of training progression and to simultaneously prepare for three weeks of development ahead. Furthermore, another tapering off of training takes place before a race, and the distance of the race can dictate how much time is needed for reduction of mileage. Faster-paced, shorter-distance races can require only a few days taper, whereas a marathon can demand a full two weeks before race day. Longer-distance ultramarathons can even justify a three-week taper, depending on volume and weekly mileage. For example, a two-week taper may entail a reduction of 30 percent the initial week, with the second week consisting of a 50 percent reduction from peak mileage. If a third week is involved, then a few runs leading up to the race earlier in the week will most likely suffice. Recovery weeks every fourth week of training, coupled with a proper tapering from training leading up to the race, provides the body with the time and rest it requires to perform at the level desired.

Sleep is an essential factor between training, and for numerous reasons can be hard to come by. Mental stress from work or home, feelings of being overwhelmed, excess responsibility, and non-stop parenting can all begin to hinder the quality and duration of sleep. Running depletes energy levels, and through sleep is where we truly replenish. Falling behind on sleep accumulates, and can begin to affect performance during training. Training through periods of time with sleep deprivation eventually hinders performance and delays recovery.

It can be ironic to advocate for rest and recovery, while my philosophy is clearly pushing limits and seeking endless possibility. Remember, though, that training is a balancing act between the bodily breakdown necessary to prepare and the rest and recovery required to progress. Put emphasis on what your body responds to most. Employing necessary training concepts is how to get from where you are to where you want to go. Training is about pushing yourself to the utmost, but sometimes pulling the reins on the mind's drive, in order to provide the rest and recovery needed, is essential. Our drive and persistence stem from the mind, which not only carries us further than we dream but can jeopardize our opportunity if we fail to train wisely. Allowing the body a chance to rejuvenate and construct its strength from rest and recovery is how we officially lock in the gains and expected results from consistent training.

Training Is Individualized

There is a massive amount of science, advisable guidelines, and theories about how we should run, how we should train, and what we should take into consideration. This can get to a point where it becomes confusing. It is every runner's job to sort through the immense amount of material available and decipher what is most important for themselves. Some information may be relevant to all, and perhaps all of the information is relevant to few. To what degree we implement the abundance of subject matter into our own running career is individualized. Formulate your own ratio as to how much you need to integrate the topics of choice. This is how we translate the trials of our experimentations into our actual experience.

We should ask ourselves these two questions.

1. What is training without the overload?
2. What is training worth if we've pushed too far?

This is the range we must work within, because training, too, becomes a balancing act. It's a matter of balancing what we want out of running with what we are capable of putting into it. Reading the science is half the fight, for the challenge is learning how to convert the science into results through constant application. Each of us decides how technically or simply we wish to train. The application of training develops our foundation and, as we build upon it, we inch ourselves closer to achieving our true capabilities and greatest potential.

PART 4:

Training to Simulate Racing

"For the things we have to learn before we can do them,
we learn by doing them."

-Aristotle

CHAPTER 9:

The Essentials

Nutrition

As training progresses, we begin to learn what works and what doesn't through the process of trial and error. Training is our opportunity to not only strengthen our mind and bodies but also provides a chance to experiment with nutrition, hydration, pace, apparel, shoes, weather, and so on. The time we invest in training should not only be viewed as physical and mental strengthening but to use certain runs within our training regimen to simulate race day. I gravitate toward marathons and ultramarathons, so naturally I utilize my long runs to mimic race day and test strategies as they pertain to nutrition and hydration.

In regard to ultrarunning, it is practically mandatory to develop a race plan that includes nutrition, such as what and when to eat, as well as a plan for hydration that includes electrolyte replacement. The intricacy of nutrition and hydration is immense, and the complexity extends as far parallel as the distances being run. Having a plan can be a start, but if it hasn't been tested and proven to work several times during training, it may not be the best individualized plan for race day. All races will not go according to plan, but a race without a plan can be a complete disaster. I personally like to know that what I consume will sit well in my stomach, is easy to digest, and provides me the energy necessary for accomplishment. Through a nutrition and hydration strategy, we are provided the essential fluid and energy needed to get from start to finish in the most efficient way. It would be comforting to know our selections have been tried and tested, time and time again through training, to alleviate any uncertainty with regard to these crucial components.

Nutrition is one of those topics that an entire, dedicated book can be written about. This book wasn't meant to elaborate on the specifics of nutrition but rather to emphasize the fact that training is an opportunity to learn about ourselves in this regard. The variety of dietary strategies available for running can range from one extreme to the other. It's to the point where they actually begin to conflict with one another, making my head spin between advice and confusion. High-carb and low-fat, high-fat and low-carb, the ketogenic diet, primal versus vegan, or even diets that vary from pescatarian to fruitarian. They all sound persuasive, as each diet has the science and research to support their ideas, plus a vast number of successful personal accounts. However, it only proves that we must experiment and come up with our own conclusions based on the immense amount of information available at our fingertips.

In any case, we will need to experiment with nutrition throughout training, if the race we are training for dictates the necessity of caloric consumption. If so, we must implement nutrition into our training and experiment with what to ingest to meet fueling demands. Energy consumption on the run is completely different than eating while at rest. The food that agrees with us at rest may not necessarily be the same food we can stomach while running. Furthermore, a half or full marathon requires a completely different nutrition plan than an ultramarathon lasting all day and into the night.

With regard to nutrition, I utilize my training to remove all doubt. If there are any questions about which diet to explore, it is paramount to experiment throughout the duration of training and during the actual training runs as well. What and when to eat on the run are questions that need to be addressed during training in order to remove all doubt once race day approaches. Not having the slightest idea isn't a chance you want to take. Nausea, and the inability to keep down food can be a runner's worst nightmare. This is especially true during ultramarathon races where energy replenishment is practically essential to continue.

Being able to consume energy while running in ninety-degree heat, when dehydration, fatigue, and exhaustion are strong possibilities, can affect your ability to give yourself the energy replenishment necessary to maintain performance. Furthermore, just because your previous race's nutrition plan, which was run in cooler weather, turned out to be successful doesn't necessarily imply the same plan will work during the ninety-degree heat scenario. Having a nutrition plan that has been tried and tested several times during training in race-like conditions, as well as having a back-up plan should the primary plan fall through, is one step closer to success than not having a plan at all. As the years pass and my training progresses, so does my nutritional experimentation. What has worked for me in the past doesn't necessarily guarantee success in the future. As I grow and evolve as a runner, so does my overall experience and knowledge with regard to the topic of nutrition, how it relates to this sport, and the affect it has on my overall performance.

Hydration and Electrolyte Balance

Maintaining adequate hydration is the attempt to replenish the volume of fluid lost through sweat during periods of exertion. On the other hand, hyponatremia is a decrease in sodium concentration caused by excess water intake, possibly by overhydrating during a race. Dehydration stems from insufficient fluid consumption, which occurs when losing more fluid than you are taking in. Everyone has a varying sweat rate, which can also largely depend on the temperatures and climates you tend to run in. The ability to sweat is simply the body's way of cooling itself, and occurs by drawing blood from the muscles toward the skin. The specific volume of necessary hydration can differ from person to person, and therefore is another topic that requires personal experience and experimentation throughout training.

Running in the heat not only increases the body's internal core temperature more quickly than running in cooler conditions but requires the cooling mechanism (sweating capability) to kick in more aggressively, redirecting a fraction of blood flow toward the skin and away from the working muscles. This is why the heat has a direct impact on the pace you are able to sustain and why digestion becomes increasingly more difficult when running in these conditions. The digestive system, working muscles, and necessary cooling system all struggle for fresh delivery of oxygenated blood. The brain will prioritize this appropriately, and cooling the internal body temperature over digestion and muscle work becomes the necessary option and safety measure. Through sweat, the body not only loses fluid but the essential electrolytes (ions) that assist with muscle contraction.

This section is not necessarily about how much or how little to drink but more about different methods of rehydration, which can contribute to finding your own personal strategy. It's hard to state what each runner needs to drink, when they should drink, and how much to consume. It makes more sense to share my experience and introduce various options and strategies that can simply be taken into consideration. But before diving into the variety of hydration methods and how to implement them, it's necessary to explore, on a superficial level, the importance of electrolytes and why they are essential.

Electrolytes play a vital role in transmitting nerve impulses for muscle contraction, as well as controlling blood pressure and volume, and maintaining the water/acid-base balance. Electrolytes include sodium, potassium, calcium, chloride, phosphate, and magnesium. Fluid and electrolytes lost through sweat requires replenishment, especially during longer-duration races and/or running in warmer temperatures. Electrolyte imbalance can cause performance to suffer, and possibly contribute to muscular cramping or fatigue, stomach cramps, and even mental confusion. Fluid and electrolyte balance are important to regulate, and can be vital to maintain not only sport performance but overall safety.

Drinking plain water to rehydrate will replenish fluid loss, however it does nothing toward electrolyte replacement or caloric intake. A sport drink not only replenishes lost fluid but can also provide energy from carbohydrates, fat, and protein. Depending on the brand, it can even include essential vitamins and electrolyte replacement. A sport drink can be a quick way to digest calories as opposed to eating solid food, which requires time and energy for the body to digest. A benefit to the powdered form of a sport drink is the ability to regulate the amount mixed in water, which can be done according to what your stomach tolerates at the time of consumption.

Compare sport drink nutrition labels to discover which may best accommodate your needs. If the sport drink of choice is one to mix in plain water, modifying the amount mixed results in a higher or lower concentration of nutrients, and will depend on what your stomach can withstand during constant motion such as running. Some sport drinks are pre-made and ready to drink after purchase. In this case, alternating the sport drink with water could stagger sugar intake, which could alleviate the risk of stomach discomfort if irritable or sensitive to sugar. If consumption of a sport drink is completely out of the question, utilizing electrolyte replacement packets or tablets to dissolve in plain water is a means of eliminating sugar from hydration altogether. If choosing that route, there is the additional factor of having to consume more calories through nutrition due to the fact that electrolyte replacement packets or tablets within plain water offer no caloric value. Though it's essential to replace fluid and electrolytes, the sport drink is what carries the additional benefit of sneaking in calories. The advantage also includes the fact that liquid is the absolute fastest method of digesting calories when energy is needed.

Between the combinations of plain water, sport drinks that contain calories and electrolytes, and electrolyte supplementation packets or tablets in plain water, there should be more than enough to experiment with and find a solution that works for you. This is where training can simulate racing, as hydration is another crucial topic to practice and experiment with prior to race day. Any questions or concerns with hydration and electrolyte replenishment can be run through the simulator during training, eventually eliminating trial and error when leading up to the actual race. When the all-important race approaches, it is comforting to know that you now have dialed into a nutrition/hydration plan consisting of what and when to eat and drink, which contributes to success and removes unnecessary anxiety that can arise from not having a plan at all.

Apparel and Equipment

It may sound absurd, but knowing exactly what to wear on race day is essential. Waking up on the day of a big race and not knowing exactly what clothing to wear can be a big mistake. What's more absurd than incorporating apparel into a race plan is having the clothing be physically irritating during the race because it hasn't been tried or tested during training. Clothing can either irritate or prevent chafing the skin, and it's best to discover this sooner rather than later. Repetitive rubbing of the skin, especially in hotter temperatures, creates friction, and friction creates heat. This produces a mild burn (chafe) unless anti-chafe is applied in areas of the skin prone to chafing. This can be extremely painful, but a valuable lesson and one that's better to experience during training than a race. Blisters on the feet or toes can form, depending on the friction within the shoe or the amount of moisture built up in the socks. It is in your best interest to have discovered and exposed these problematic areas during training to decrease the chances of issues arising on race day.

Apparel has a broader sense of meaning to me, as it pertains to everything worn from head to toe. The selection of compression or loose-fitting clothing, a proper-fitting hat and pair of sunglasses, and the appropriate pair of running shoes and socks make all the difference in the world. This goes for the trust we place in any gear and equipment we expect to rely on, such as headlamps, blinking lights, a GPS running watch, trekking poles, and even hydration packs. Though it may sound obvious, nothing could be worse than beginning a race and realizing the headlamp doesn't work or the bladder within the hydration pack leaks. Utilize training to reveal exactly what to trust absolutely.

I utilize my long runs each week to begin testing nutrition and hydration strategies, and I begin wearing exactly what I will be during my race. Replicating race strategy as closely as possible simulates race day, leaving less guesswork as the ultimate challenge nears. When the important day arrives, it's even more soothing to know exactly what to wear from head to toe. Nailing down the three components of nutrition, hydration, and apparel is crucial, and can reduce potential problems in the future.

The pre-race early morning ritual is wearing, eating, and drinking the exact same things as on the mornings of long runs and, because it's more of a routine, it eliminates unnecessary stress and anxiety. If there are any remaining questions concerning these topics, either they haven't been tested enough or something different requires testing. All of these questions should be run through the simulator (training) enough that the answers become clear. These are topics you need assurance on once the race date arrives. There is no reason you should leave any of these variables, which are completely in your control, unexamined.

Aside from testing the components of nutrition, hydration, and apparel, it's important to begin introducing the stress you may encounter on race day. I find it helpful to simulate a race by using back-to-back long runs and a two-a-day approach. Furthermore, the addition of periodic strengthening sessions before running, which accelerates the fatigue, moved the late-race feeling toward the beginning of our workout. The more you simulate and take advantage of the conditions you may be exposed to on race day, the higher your chances are to succeed and conquer the goal you have set out to accomplish.

CHAPTER 10:

Apply and Execute

Back-to-Back Long Runs and the Two-a-Day Approach

One key to training is to remain specific and attempt to replicate your race as much as possible. Once I progress in training to where weekly mileage dictates running more frequently, it's also the time to toss in back-to-back long runs or two-a-day workouts. This carries a dual purpose, as it's not only a beneficial method of increasing weekly mileage but also closer simulates what it will feel like to compress a high volume of running within a short period of time. The following training methods will not only apply more stress on the body but will test the mind's overall willingness for the challenge.

When the volume of weekly mileage is ready for a boost, begin to incorporate back-to-back long runs if the body can readily absorb this stress. Consider implementing this on the first and third weeks of a training month. Week one is coming off a recovery week and week three is concluded by entering another recovery week. The second week can be supported by a few two-workout days of lower mileage to maintain the volume. Easing back on the pace during these two long runs is a way to mitigate the additional risk from the higher volume of mileage in a forty-eight-hour period.

The weekly long run is now joined by yet another long run the following day. The feelings of exhaustion, followed by the muscle soreness and fatigue, will only become more subtle if you push past it and run with that very same feeling. A long run can drain the mind and body, especially when it follows multiple days of training leading up to it. This is the point where that feeling is what you bring into a subsequent long run. This forces the mind and body to grow accustomed to expanding your perceived limitations and accept the fact that you are pushing through barriers. It will be tough to progress if you rest when you're tired. We must constantly find balance by pushing when you must and resting when you can.

Though back-to-back long runs are directed toward distance training, both long-distance runners and those who incorporate speed can utilize the two-a-day approach. Avoid two high-intensity runs within the same day, as it's more beneficial to include one run at higher intensity and the second run that day at recovery pace. Be sure the body can handle the stress load prior to incorporating back-to-back long runs or two-a-day workouts. These benefits are not worth the consequences of introducing bodily stress prematurely.

The two-a-day approach serves multiple purposes: they can boost your weekly mileage and accustom the mind and body to running more frequently. If ready to implement, be sure to stagger the two-workout days throughout the length of the week, as opposed to doing two or three days with multiple work-outs in the beginning or end of the week. Remember, increasing frequency too quickly within a small timeframe only increases risk and isn't worth a setback at this point in time. Maintain the balance of mileage throughout the week to allow yourself ample time for recovery. Another benefit to running twice in one day, or even back-to-back long runs, is that the second run can help you recover from the first.

Following a tough workout with a second run at aerobic pace can speed recovery by flushing muscle soreness through the muscle contractions. At times, it can be more beneficial for recovery to run than to lie around all day not promoting circulation. Muscle contractions facilitate blood flow (oxygenated red blood cells), which increases circulation and aids in muscle recovery. This process can flush out muscle soreness that may have accumulated from a previous hard workout. Allowing muscle soreness to linger only delays its departure, which is why active recovery, or a run at aerobic pace, can actually aid or speed your recovery. Again, this must be at a time when the body can handle the additional mileage, and the following run should be at recovery pace to avoid causing any additional damage. We want to facilitate recovery, not impede the process of repair.

Be sure to implement this slowly, with caution, and only if these workouts are specific to your training goals and endeavors. Being creative is part of training and, as we progress and excel as runners, we need to find ways to obtain and sufficiently increase frequency, intensity, and duration. It's important to implement the progress into our schedules in a balanced manner in order to ensure safety and a healthy arrival at the start. Training progression begins to require more time, so it's important to continue to remain balanced in life, and that the decisions made within training are safe and responsible.

Strengthening before Running

The longer the duration of a race, the more your muscles need to withstand the pounding. How can we mimic what our legs will feel like late in the race if we begin each training run fresh and recovered? I utilize strength training not only for the benefits previously stated but to break down and weaken the muscles before running to closely mimic late-race feelings. Toward the end of the race, your legs will feel a lot different than when you first began. If your legs are unfamiliar with running when fatigued, then the expectation of your legs performing when faced with fatigue is simply unrealistic.

Strengthening is a way to not only address weaknesses and muscular imbalance, but is one way to move your muscles closer to fatigue. Remember that as we perform strengthening exercises, we are breaking down muscle tissue and, therefore, are actually getting weaker in the process. How can we perceive this as advantageous? Forcing your legs to run following a strengthening session that places them in a weakened state can teach valuable lessons not found when constantly training on freshly recovered legs. Implementing this strategy in the middle of a training week can help to steer clear of weekend long runs and create a balance of the stress you're enduring throughout a seven-day workload.

Bringing the muscles to a point of fatigue, where running seems to be out of the question, has now become the focal point of this particular challenge. It's not an illogical workout if I'm ultimately asking my muscles to perform for twelve to twenty-four hours straight in order to complete an ultramarathon. The beginning of the run will lack muscle coordination and control, as the strength your muscles had before this session has been mostly extracted. Running without strength in your legs is the exact reason for this workout, as training should continue to provide simulations and familiarizations with the race itself.

During the last quarter of your race, when your legs are feeling heavy or as if the strength has been extracted from your muscles, it will occur to you that you've simulated this in the past and have prevailed. Those strength workouts right before your training run are just another way of catapulting you to what it may feel like toward the end of a race. What good would it be if you always continued to train on fresh legs, which is only what the first half of the race will actually feel like? I am not saying to choose this method over any other, it is simply another idea to incorporate into your training once a week or every other week for the reason stated. To run strong on weak legs, we must first practice the weakening of our legs and teach them to run strong.

Disregarding Inclement Weather

Another way to acclimate yourself with race conditions can be through the exposure to anticipated weather. It is easy to find the average temperatures for the race you register for, but that doesn't say much about whether it will include rain throughout the entire race, a torrential downpour, or snow for those who live outside of South Florida. Canceling training runs because it is raining eliminates opportunity to simulate what it feels like to run in the rain. If you have only trained in optimal conditions and have not accustomed yourself to training in the rain or heat, how can you expect your body to perform under those particular conditions?

I have run many marathons and ultramarathons in the pouring rain, not necessarily out of choice but because I don't get to choose race-day conditions. I have run many marathons and ultramarathons in ninety-degree heat, and not necessarily by choice but because that was the temperature on race day. I strongly, but safely, suggest getting those training runs in regardless of weather, because you never know what you will encounter on actual race day. You need to include weather conditions and temperatures in the specifics of training for adaptation purposes, which will strongly increase your odds of success and completing the goal you set out to accomplish. Some runners need to acclimate themselves to altitude by running at higher elevations, which may require the incorporation of encountered race-day ascent/descent into their training. If running a trail race, obviously spend more time trail running. If it is a road race, then hit the pavement and grow accustomed to what that feels like. These are obvious ideas to address, but some neglect the thought of temperature, weather, or terrain.

Your busy schedule may require training runs early in the morning before the sun comes up. However, if the race you are training for reaches temperatures upward of ninety degrees Fahrenheit with a high humidity factor, it is more beneficial to occasionally train mid-day, when temperatures are closer to reaching ninety degrees. If you are training for an ultramarathon that may last all day and into the night, try running at night to familiarize yourself with that particular dynamic. Running at the very end of the day, or at night when your energy levels are lower, can add diversification and become more beneficial than training at the same time each day.

Training is sometimes thought of as unidimensional, that its sole purpose is to strengthen your body sufficiently to carry you through and achieve your goal. The main point I am making throughout this section is that training is so much more than getting out there and grinding out the miles. Training is about maximizing the time spent running; to conduct the necessary experimentation with nutrition, hydration/electrolytes, apparel, weather, and temperatures; and even the variety of training methods you respond to best. The mental challenge of facing components of adversity, such as inclement weather or extreme temperatures, leads to self-confidence and reassurance since they are prior experiences. It is precisely how you can eliminate any lingering questions about these topics. If your outlook and perspective have shifted into how to make training multi-purpose, it will equate to running time well spent. This results in a larger return on your investment of time, and a higher level of achievement and success.

Test Your Race with a Race

Taking advantage of a race during training can not only test your progress but can expose weaker areas that may require improvement. The strategic placement of a race during training can also provide a necessary assessment of how your training is progressing. The race you run midway through training doesn't entail the same distance, or even the same speed, as the end-goal but provides the opportunity to test race-day strategy and exposes areas to place emphasis on during training. The reinforcement of weaker areas can increase performance substantially.

The placement and timing of a test race is critical during training, because you will want enough time to adequately prepare for it. Training can bring about thoughts of whether or not you are on track, and without a test race to provide this crucial feedback there can be fewer indicators to say otherwise. Running a test race will answer that question because it will show you if the pace is sustainable, your time was on track, the nutrition and hydration are dialed in, and areas of training you would like to fine tune. It is an opportunity to make your mistakes, if need be, and make the necessary tweaks and adjustments, or it could be the reassurance needed to remain on track.

When you resume training following the test race, you will have a different outlook and focus than if you had not run that race. Although the trial run will not be the same distance as your end goal, it helps provide you with the repetition and execution of your plan. For example, if you are training for a marathon, running a half marathon or two leading up to the actual marathon helps you execute your first-half strategies. It is also important to acknowledge how you feel when you reach the finish. Hitting your pace and target time is a good sign, however, the other indicator is how you feel. Do you feel you could have continued or did you feel on the verge of collapse?

When I train for an ultramarathon, I usually climb the ladder of distances as I progress through training. Training for a fifty-miler compels me to run a marathon or a fifty-kilometer race (50K—thirty-one miles) before arriving at the fifty-mile start. Training for a 100-miler further compels me to factor in a marathon or a 50K, or even a fifty-miler leading up to the race. This exposes what works and what doesn't, provides an opportunity to experiment with any new strategies, and highlights whether I am on track to accomplish what I have ultimately committed to do.

Each year of running is another year of experience, which includes enhanced mental and physical strength, and the additional knowledge brought upon through trial and error. I evolve as a runner by continuing to learn more about my mind and body. Each year I incorporate what I have learned in the past, with the experimentation I am currently conducting, to emerge as a mentally and physically stronger runner than the previous couple of years. The training is a tool that gets us from where we are to where we want to go. When the moment arrives and we stand at the starting line, it is up to us to apply and execute the training we have put ourselves through. Trust the fact that everything you have invested your energy in will be worth the satisfaction you gain through the successful completion and accomplishment of your goal.

Trust Your Training

When race day arrives, it may bring about feelings that you didn't train hard enough or that you could have done a bit more. A little more strengthening, higher weekly mileage, even a thought that your long run two weeks ago wasn't far enough. Those who have the drive to push through training are the same people who want to squeeze every last ounce out of themselves. The truth is that we more than likely did everything we could. We have diligently sacrificed our time and energy for several months in succession, pushed ourselves on mornings or evenings we didn't feel up for the work, bypassed the lack of sleep and energy deprivation, and constantly removed ourselves from the comfort of stagnation. Strengthening and conditioning the mind and body for four to six months is a tremendous investment. It is time to trust our training and acknowledge that the process wasn't easy and prepared us for the opportunity for success that lies ahead.

Do we have what it takes to succeed? There is a balance between remaining humble and having confidence. Humility is important and keeps us hypervigilant, which contributes to our overall success. It's intimidating to attempt a new distance never run before, and ironically requires confidence to keep your head in the game when things become difficult. However, being overly confident or outright arrogant is also problematic, and could lead to mistakes and failure along the way. This could lead to improper pacing, neglect of potential issues, or not fully respecting the distance being attempted. Regardless of the distance being run, it will always be challenging if you push beyond capacity. Somewhere in between humility and confidence is a balance worth exploring.

Once you have run out of time to train, it boils down to placing trust in the training you have endured. You know the exact pace you will run, what and when to eat, your hydration and electrolyte strategies, apparel from head to toe, and all the questions have been answered after being run through the simulator. You have accustomed yourself to running in like temperatures, at the right times, and in all sorts of different weather conditions. You have familiarized yourself as much as possible to what this race will feel like. Getting to the starting line healthily equipped was your number-one priority, and now getting to the finish line is the number-one objective. Handling what the race throws your way is what you've prepared for, you just don't know what event that will be. There is always excitement of the unknown, however, you have the capabilities to prevail and the mindset to back it up. Trusting your training prior to the race is the confidence you have in the training you've done. This will not only negate a percentage of the anxiety prior to the race but will also contribute to your overall success throughout the entire journey.

Summation of Forces

Preliminary training consists of preparation, the willingness to invest your time and energy, and instilling the proper mindset to fulfill the goal you have ultimately committed to. The application of training conditions the mind and body for the challenge you have bestowed upon yourself. Running and cross-training are focal points while incorporating injury prevention and safety along the way. Nutrition and hydration strategies, apparel, equipment use, and training in race-like conditions have all been executed in several trial runs or even test races. You have even begun increasing bodily stress with back-to-back long runs and two-workout days to replicate race demand, and incorporated strength training before running to grow accustomed to fatigue, all of which familiarizes your body with late-race feelings. When all said and done, you have taken full advantage of specificity and the overload principle.

What else can you do but show up to the race, with a force you have created just waiting for release. The potential energy you have built after training will be transferred into kinetic energy and, upon release, will turn your motion into momentum. Force summation is the force produced when all of your muscles act simultaneously and in combination. Therefore, you can produce a much more powerful force when all of your muscles combine than the force each muscle can produce individually. Your training is a way of producing that force and, when put together in combination with your mindset, will produce a much greater force than originally expected. You have every right to start your race with confidence, as there is no better option than to trust in your training and the power of your mind.

PART 5:

Running Ultra

"Only those who risk going too far, can possibly find out how far one can go."

-T.S. Eliot

CHAPTER 11:

Free to Run Far

Why Run Ultra?

The most basic definition of an ultramarathon is any distance longer than the traditional 26.2-mile marathon. Ultramarathons can be fifty kilometers (31 miles), fifty miles, 100 kilometers (62 miles), and 100 miles. There are plenty of events that go well beyond the 100-mile distance in a single push or multi-stage. I think it's fair for people to ask why runners would push themselves to these extreme measures. I have been asked this question many times before, as this why question has stemmed from sheer curiosity, confusion, and even repulsion. While every runner has their own specific reasoning, I can only answer this question on my own behalf.

When asked why, my simple answer is to challenge myself, and because of the fact that it isn't socially acceptable to become philosophical when circumstances demand short answers. However, there is much more to the answer. Sometimes, getting through my day at work is a challenge. Other times, just leaving the house to go to work is a challenge, with two small boys requiring copious amounts of attention during morning routines. There are so many facets of my everyday life that can be labeled as challenging that I wouldn't need to run more than 100 miles just to simply challenge myself. There is so much more to the explanation when answering what seems like a simple question.

I have spoken of the journey I am on, the pursuit of seeking true capability. Through running longer distances, I have discovered I have untapped potential yearning for discovery. True potential lies beyond perceived limitations, and pushing through these barriers can unlock hidden strength that would otherwise be left untouched. I run ultramarathons because they offer an opportunity to satisfy the curiosity I have within, of whether there are limitations or endless possibilities. Ultramarathons reveal clarity, not only with regard to where true potential lies but how much more there is to unlock. I run ultramarathons not only for the challenge but for the sake of opportunity and a deeper self-awareness.

Running has engrained in me a limitless philosophy, that the human mind is capable of more than we imagine. I have a drive to discover my greatest potential and seek to overcome what is deemed impossible. I pursue and chase what lies beyond, and uncover who I am in the depths of my character. Distance peels away physical, mental, and emotional layers of self, which exposes a genuine vulnerability and nothing to shield or protect myself with. I am driven to understand how to grow as a person through repetitious cycles of challenge and success. As reasonable as it sounds to inquire why I run the way that I do, it is equally logical to pose the inverse of the very same question. So, why would I not?

The Race Begins at our Breaking Point

Every race has a consistent starting point. The official starting line begins the race at the same location from one runner to the next. Once we cross over that line, we immediately begin decreasing the distance remaining between ourselves and the finish. Time continues to increase, and will do so at a steady and constant rate regardless of how fast or slow we advance. Depending on the distance, we may arrive at the finish line in a couple of hours or we may not finish until tomorrow. Everyone has the same goal in mind, to eventually cross that finish line. The times in which they do so will vary, but what everyone who finishes has in common is the respectable distance they've covered.

Distance can never change, only the amount of time required to cover it. No matter how fast or slow the pace, there is mutual respect when we run the same unimaginable distance.

My impression is that there are two starting lines during an ultramarathon, the official one that we initially cross and the imaginary one that lies somewhere in an unknown location. When we cross the initial starting line, we are physically at our strongest and mentally at our toughest. Our bodies have yet to begin breaking down and the impact of running hasn't begun to compile. Mental excitement is present as we begin our quest for personal accomplishment. But over time and as the race unfolds, the distance eventually wears on the mind and body until we reach what's considered a breaking point. The race has become the challenge it was meant to be, and this is where I theorize the race actually begins.

The breaking point could simply mean being stripped of the physical, mental, and emotional aspects of self. The longer the race, the more breaking points lie ahead, and the more difficult it may become to persevere. It's not to say that the distance run before this point didn't accumulate or amount to anything, for that is the distance it took to bring us to this state. It took those miles, at that pace, in those specific conditions and temperatures, to bring us to where we currently stand. Reaching the halfway point of a fifty-mile race is practically running a full marathon, and regardless of the runner's condition it will take running almost another marathon just to officially finish. Perhaps the runner's condition is no better than having to occasionally vomit from hours of nausea, while temperatures are beginning to reach ninety degrees Fahrenheit. This can make for a pretty daunting start to the second half of a very long race.

This is where our minds are put to the test. You see, other people aren't the only ones that ask why I run ultramarathons. There are times during a race when I ask myself this very same question. The question comes in many different forms and from many different angles, but in the end it is a question I'm sure every runner will eventually come to terms with. While being in the worst condition during a race isn't the most convenient time for this particular question, it arrives when we least expect it to and is simply measuring our level of commitment. These are the moments when having a meaning and purpose will prevail. Preliminary training required self-reflection, understanding of our own reasoning and purpose, the meaning as to why we are choosing the goal we've chosen. It may not have been obvious or apparent at the time, but this is why it's important to have settled this question before reaching the starting line. Like an ace of spades, we wait for the right moment to play it. We won't have to decide when, because the situation we're in will invariably demand it.

Are these breaking points barriers that we must push through, perceived limitations that must be penetrated to gain exposure into the unknown? To unlock this so-called true potential, you may assume that a special key is needed. But the real key is having a proper mindset, which lies in consistency of self-discipline and sacrifice. Great accomplishments don't come easily, and I believe the biggest achievements and fulfillment of success can be found through voluntary challenges that we initiate ourselves. Mentally, we can drive our bodies beyond capability, we just have to be physically willing to accept that. The pain we endure is temporary, but the impression it makes is etched in our character. Breaking points are opportunities and should be sought after, not run from. Not only is that where the real challenge begins, but the moment where we uncover our true strength and hidden potential.

The Perception of Extreme Distances

Over the years, I have begun to look at distance differently. I remember thinking that some distances are just too big to even think about. I was still at a point where the marathon overwhelmed me. When I began venturing into the 50K and fifty-mile distances, it began to change my perception on the marathon. Though running a 26.2-mile marathon is a far distance and challenging to the utmost, my view and perspective toward it had changed. Ultramarathons have taught me how to mentally dismantle distances into smaller, more feasible chunks, making the overall outlook on extreme distances manageable. Physically, there is no changing distance. The fifty-mile distance will always be a distance of fifty miles. However, what could begin to change distance is our mental approach and how we perceive it.

The 50K and fifty-mile distances are of a completely different caliber, and every mistake is amplified to be more costly due to the remaining distance that lay ahead. Experience came with a price, but a price worth paying for future investment. Even if previous mistakes are never repeated, there is always a new set of mistakes to be made. Learning over the years has provided me with experience I couldn't otherwise obtain. The 50K and fifty-mile race has a very special place in my mind with regard to my perception of extreme distances. They were my introduction to ultra, and acted as a median between my overall perception on the marathon and my fascination with running the 100-mile distance. This new perspective allowed me to look ahead and actually entertain the idea of attempting a 100-miler.

Strolling in from finishing a few fifty-mile races, I began to wonder if a greater distance was possible for an average runner like myself. Each of these races seemed to chew me up and spit me out, yet I remained open to the fact that there is more to be discovered. I was beginning to catch a glimpse of opportunity, and I wondered to myself if it was time. I have never even come close to winning a race. However, I take pride in knowing I've never lost a fight despite insurmountable odds that were stacked against me. Knowing my level of determination to seek what ultrarunning has to offer, my perception changed from not knowing if I could ever accomplish a 100-mile race to wanting a fair shot and being ready to attempt one. This new mindset changed my views toward previous races and the future goals I would eventually pursue.

As my ambitions escalate, so does the distance of my overall journey. What begins to expand alongside my aspirations are the distant horizons needed to accommodate them. My peripheral vision widens. The horizon and vast amounts of distance are really just my perception of extreme distances and what the sport of ultrarunning has to offer. I have become open-minded to the unceasing opportunity, as this is the only way to describe the direction of my journey. Where ever this is heading is the direction I'm going.

Patience Pays

From the moment we start our race, the clock begins to tick against us and applies constant pressure, putting patience to the test. This psychological pressure and anxiety can derive from nothing more than our own impatience. Succumbing to this feeling can cause us to speed up, and the belief that doing so will relieve this anxiety is simply an illusion. It's tough to measure a feeling of pressure that haunts us for a couple dozen hours in non-stop fashion. The constant mental calculation, of how much to push and how conservative to remain, is a mental tug-of-war for the duration of each race. A plan that includes appropriate pacing and time can help maintain mental focus and avoid possible errors. Deviating from the plan early on can result in a miserable second half of the race, and risks forfeiting the time goal we are aiming to shoot for.

There is just no cheating an ultramarathon. Outpacing ourselves early in the race will permit the distance to catch up and halt us in our tracks. There is too much distance left to cover to remain unscathed from costly error. The race course seems to have the advantage when we give in to this pressure and level of impatience. There is no doubt about it, ultrarunning requires loads of forbearance. No matter the level of expertise, anyone can miscalculate their pace and attempt to run at unsustainable efforts. An unsustainable level of exertion can only be maintained for a certain distance and for a certain amount of time. A misjudgment, or falling short of being patient, will only result in consequences and demonstrate the importance for reserve. These mistakes have served as brutal learning curves, but have also proven worthwhile in the grand scheme. I have learned to improve upon my level of patience for the necessary lengths of time required.

Discipline is required to stick to a plan. To save yourself during the first half, solely to prepare for the second, sounds a bit counter-productive when pumped with adrenaline and feelings of euphoria. Trying to maximize this so-called conservative and sustainable pace is one of the many challenges and beauties of ultrarunning. Distances of 50 to 100 miles are very long distances, and there is no way around it. I understand the clock is ticking, but with too much distance out in front it only makes errors that much more costly. *It's still early*, is a mantra I use throughout the race, regardless of the distance I've put behind me. If I feel physically and mentally refreshed at mile forty, that is the reason to remind myself *It's still early*. This mantra brings patience to the present moment when a substantial distance remains to be covered.

Problem-solving, an important aspect of ultrarunning, requires many calculated risks to be made without any sure way of knowing the best possible outcome. We cannot know if a decision we're forced to make will hinder our race or become a mistake. Sometimes the options don't offer great outcomes. Problems will arise during long-distance races. How we go about managing them is either advantageous or detrimental. We have to make decisions and take calculated risks. Sometimes choosing the less-risky and more time-consuming option is an opportune time to exercise patience. There is no way of knowing if the decisions made will be correct until the race continues to reveal itself. Sometimes it is best to not allow time to be the sole factor in our decision-making process.

Through proper training, strategizing, and the discipline to stick to a plan, we can begin to reduce the margin of error. *Run your race* means stick to your plan. During an ultra, it can be impossible to judge how others have trained, what their experience level is, the distances they've seen, or how their genetic make-up is comprised. There will be a variety of ultrarunners running that race, and it can be easy to get sucked into a pace that is inevitably unsustainable for you. I stick to my plan and I run my race. I stick to a regimented plan during the first half and go completely by feel during the second half of the race.

My longest run during training usually entails about half the distance of my ultimate goal. I simply do not incorporate an eighty-mile training run to prepare for a 100-mile race. The recovery would be too strenuous and only impede on the remaining portion of training. The preparation for a 100-mile race dictates a plan that includes running a fifty-miler or 100K as my longest training run. For this reason, it would be impossible for me to plan out, in detail, everything the second half of the race might entail. Committing to a regimented plan for a second half of the race I have been completely unexposed to only increases chances of mounting frustration and mental fatigue. The plan for the remaining fifty miles will likely begin to fall apart and may decrease the likelihood of success if I continue to force a plan that requires a change. Going by feel allows me to be open-minded to making the changes and modifications necessary to complete a race and a goal of this magnitude.

I spend the first half of my race setting the stage for a successful ending. It is laying down the structure, foundation, and groundwork for a stronger and more effective second half of the race. Sometimes this means sticking to my plan and running my race, and other times it means exercising patience along the way. Patience may seem like it's working against us, but the payoff comes as we're nearing the end. Having patience is running a smart race. "Pay me now, or pay me later" says the distance to the time it takes to eventually complete it.

Happy to Start, Happy to Finish

There always seems to be excitement building as I near a big race, and, when the time arrives, it's the moment I have prepared for. There has been extensive sacrifice and dedication along the way. Much has been poured into the preparation and training as I attempt to accomplish one single race. The day has come, and I stand at the starting line. A moment of realization sets in. The countdown begins and I am now in the process of decreasing the mileage that lies between me and the finish line. That finish line could be fifty miles away, or incomprehensibly, it could be 100. Although it's exciting to begin a race, it will be a very long day, and perhaps a more grueling night.

I'm always happy to start a race, but, ironically, I'm just as happy to see the finish. The truth is that a lot goes on between the start and the finish. The distance of the race does not sustain the excitement I feel at the start. In fact, it will inevitably strip it away at one point or another and introduce the reality of circumstantial difficulty. Observe the start and finish of any race and you will see runners who are happy to start and happy to finish. But the journey happens between those two lines. What would a start be without a finish, and what would a finish be without the struggle to arrive?

The journey can include every single emotion, ranging from complete elation to total despair. Everything from extreme highs to severe lows, the peaks and valleys of emotions to endure. So, we move forward as best we can, sometimes running and sometimes walking. These feelings may last a matter of minutes, or could even last several hours. The mind is talking, but listening is optional. What is the reasoning behind this fight? It's very easy to start a race, and quite the opposite to actually finish. The training is done, but the real challenge remains. Regardless of what stands in the way, a mountain to climb or fifty miles to run, we learn to dig deep and get the job done.

Each mile run is one less in front. Every step taken is one less required. I was excited to begin, yet anxious to finish. Distance and time are mere opponents, with tricks of their own, their capabilities unmatched. While distance is finite and seems to sit still, time is infinite and seems to keep moving. Challenged by the fatigable mind and body, neither of these opponents will ever grow tired. Does this irony lure human endurance, fighting tireless opponents with fatigable ability?

These are the challenges I tend to seek and the moments that I tend to embrace. Easy to say but difficult to do, this is what I've committed myself to. The ability to break through those moments of despair, when the odds were against me and everything looked unfavorable. Back against the wall without a shield for protection, mentally combating what remains out front. The battle that stands between me and the finish makes a worthy fulfillment and humble success. It's recognized as happy to start and happy to finish, the same expression for contrary reasoning. Through training, we have earned for ourselves the right to start, but the finish was earned through the fight to survive.

CHAPTER 12:

The Journey Begins

The 100-Mile Distance

Since the time I began running marathons, I have enjoyed reading books about ultramarathon running. I would read about the 100-mile distance and wonder if it was possible for someone like myself, a mid-pack runner with average finishing times, to even begin to consider. I read about these extreme distances and was under the impression that, while it may be applicable to some runners these races didn't apply to people like me. As it was, I still found the marathon as challenging as it was overwhelming. I continued to read about ultrarunning, and continued to ponder the thought of this becoming my reality. After running numerous marathons and learning painful lessons, I entertained the idea of running my first ultra.

No matter how fast or slow we take it, distance has ways of catching up with us. It seems to taunt our every emotion, disintegrate our physical state, and disrupt our mental status. Ultramarathons began to change my perception of the traditional marathon, but more importantly they opened my mind to attempting the 100-mile distance. Once I began to entertain this idea, it widened my peripheral views and I began to envision the opportunity with clarity. It removed the horse blinders I was oblivious to wearing, as it took what it took to stand where I stood. A distance of this magnitude poured fuel on the fire, and gave hope this journey wasn't close to an end. On the contrary, it was just beginning.

As I progress along the journey of my running career, my curiosity deepens and requires fulfillment. The only way to see what this sport has to offer is to arrive at a distance and experience it personally. The more my dreams become a reality, the more clarity I have in the direction I'm heading. My reasoning and pursuit in this particular direction are to gain more exposure of unfound strength. There is simply more to this distance than the distance itself.

Running 100 miles is the race that, for me, forces me to discover capabilities unknown. Although it is a very long distance and no easy feat, it is possible to all who may wonder. It would be unreasonable to sugarcoat the description, and perhaps overbearing no matter how it's explained. If you run twenty miles, there is still another eighty to go. Running forty miles leaves another sixty to go. The 100K mark, at mile sixty-two, still holds another thirty-eight miles unaccomplished. And yes, after going a whopping ninety, there are still ten miles left out on the table. Although this may be tough to fathom, this is not the mindset going into this race. This is not how to mentally approach tackling 100 miles.

Sometimes we take it one mile at a time. It can be thought of as aid-station to aid-station. It can become so rough that the focus shifts, mentally, to taking it one step at a time. After all, the only way to accomplish distance on foot is by simply putting one foot in front of the other. Who would have thought that such an easy concept can bring so much difficulty and so much strain? It's important how we mentally approach this race, not only beforehand but throughout its entirety. Mentally, it's best to break up the distance into feasible and more manageable chunks, and to attack the remaining portions in that sort of way.

If this sport was based on physical strength, then ultrarunning would count me out entirely. I have always been naturally thin, carrying only enough muscle tone to get the job done. Hypertrophy, the increase of skeletal muscle tissue, just isn't a goal of mine and never has been. Muscle mass weighs more than we think and, therefore, requires greater amounts of energy to carry. I understand that more muscle may equate to greater strength, but at what point would this become a hindrance? This is the main reason I aim for endurance and prefer it more so than training for power.

I don't pack much power or carry much strength, but instead have a strong will and sheer determination. I have an unrelenting passion for goal-setting and success. However, these are characteristics that cannot be seen. Perhaps through a passion being expressed, or when a mind is challenged and put to the test, can they suddenly become noticeable and visually apparent. It is why we can't judge a book by its cover. Late in a race, one lasting 100 miles and beyond, you won't have to look far to see the mind and heart. It is the only way to describe what I've seen and been through. There is no other explanation for what drives individuals beyond what appears to be inconceivable. Having heart is having a passion. I have the heart and am building the mindset to drive me there. The combination of passionate will can certainly push further than we ever thought possible. It is why the 100-mile race is so special and unique. Not only do I see two sunrises on the same run but it provides the mind and heart an opportunity to shine.

The Belt Buckle

As I sit and wonder how this came to be, a couple of belt buckles stare back at me. My running career began long before I knew it would become one. Crossing the starting line brings reality to the race, as does writing about a couple of belt buckles. Finisher medals jog memories of previous races, but the belt buckles tell an entirely different story. As some of you may wonder, the belt buckle is an award heavily sought after in the ultra-community. Crossing the finish line of a 100-mile endurance run earns a coveted belt buckle, customized and uniquely designed. It doesn't sound like much until experiencing what it takes to earn one.

The belt buckles sit atop my finisher medal wall mount. Each are responsible for a chapter in my story as I continue to progress through the length of my journey. One difference between the belt buckles and finisher medals is the buckles involved a team effort and entire support crew. Strengthening the bond between my support crew and me is what makes these races entirely unique. The races create memories that can't possibly be forgotten. If the bonds were strong before the race, the strength seems to nearly double. There is something unique about mutual accomplishment, a reliance on one another to conquer success. Belt buckles not only represent how far I've come in my running career but within my personal life in its entirety. The 100-mile distance exhibits many of life's lessons, such as how many small choices lead to large changes.

All of the small choices we make on a daily basis can lead to much larger changes over time. Perhaps it's the change we've always wanted to see. Covering a long distance one step at a time is comparable to the small choices we make from day to day. This eventually leads to changes we hope for and the goals we've hoped to eventually achieve. In my personal life a decade ago, I approached a fork in the road that presented the opportune time to make the changes I sought. With the help of a strong support crew, I made the decision to put distance between the struggle I was tangled in to where I currently stand.

Belt buckles not only represent a specific distance that's been run but the distance between that fork in the road and where I manage to stand today. As I hold the buckles in my hand and stare at the customized engraving, I think to myself *How did I get from point A to point B?* The answer is by having a strong support crew. Having a support crew in life and even during a 100-mile race can be significant when choosing the right people. We are the average of the five people we surround ourselves with most, so jump in the middle of those who empower you and those who support you from start to finish. I never see just a finisher medal or plain old belt buckle; I see the meaning they provide and the symbolism they bring.

To My Support Crew

Dear Support Crew,

It can be extremely difficult finding individuals with the values you share. I want to thank you for sacrificing entire weekends and countless hours of precious sleep all to help me chase and pursue a list of my dreams, goals, and unrelenting ambitions. It's not easy to find the perfect support crew, those willing to work as diligently as you. What others don't realize is everything that happens behind the scenes and, when there isn't work that has to be done, you sit with the feeling of infinite waiting. Besides all the tasks that vary along with everything the adventure seems to entail, you're with me from the very beginning until the bitter end.

I want to thank you for knowing how to push me and when to hold back. For providing mental support when things seem grim. For constantly providing me with essentials and pacing and the countless miles we've run, walked, and trudged. This includes the conversations we have had, including the ones that were memorable and those that were forgotten. For the occasional dirty joke and the absolute silence while we focus on placing one foot in front of the other. Iced-water sponge baths to cool me from the heat and blasting the heater to warm me from hypothermic conditions.

You've dealt with the roller-coaster ride of emotions, which range from extreme highs down to severe lows. You let me laugh it out and later cry, because that's what I needed at that specific time. Blister management is a deal breaker for most, but you'll even throw that one in for good measure. Having everything ready for me, in the particular ways I need it, is constant routine and work around the clock. You are either pacing, organizing, and preparing everything, or waiting, which is just as equally exhausting. How could I thank you or return these favors? Dinners and fishing trips are a start, but in the end how could I really thank you?

Without your help, dedication, and selfless sacrifice, I would not be this far along on my journey. Words cannot describe the gratitude one feels when a team of people work as hard as you do, in order to witness someone else accomplish a goal they must have thought up while consciously dreaming. I want to personally thank my crew, and the many volunteers at the races and aid-stations, for all of your selfless dedication and sacrifice. I can only continue to pay it forward because of those who have helped me get where I stand. Although my ambitious endeavors have only begun, I am eternally grateful for all that you've done.

PART 6:

The Journey Continues

"It does not matter how slowly you go as long as you never stop."

-Confucius

CHAPTER 13:

Endless Possibility

The Keys 100

In May of 2017, I embarked on my first 100-mile race, called the Keys 100. It goes from Key Largo to Key West and runs south along Overseas Highway. The Florida Keys have always been special to me throughout my life. Childhood trips consisted of barracuda and snapper fishing, swimming in the reefs, and lobstering at night with bully nets and flood lights. Born and raised in Miami, the Keys have always been a quick ride south and made for a perfect day-long visit or weekend getaway. I wanted to make my first 100-miler personal, and what better choice than to begin this race where I married my beautiful wife, Catherine, a few years earlier. I believed that providing this race with a meaning and purpose would be a motivating factor and psychological advantage.

I trained for a solid six-month period, and prepared for the heat by planning weekly long runs during the hottest portions of the day. In my case, all of the preparation in the world couldn't substitute or prepare me for a lack of experience running this distance. There is always a bodily shock when attempting a new distance for the very first time. I perspired for two days leading up to the race, strictly due to the amount of anxiety I felt. For the body to react in this sort of way during the two days leading up to this particular race shows the immense psychological impact behind the sport of ultrarunning. *Was I ready for this race? Was I ready for the distance?*

Who could have told me if I were ready or not? The training was there, my dedication and sacrifice were flawless. The only thing missing was the fact that I had never run this long a distance before. In fact, before this race, I had only run a handful of 50K and fifty-mile races over the previous couple of years. If the fifty-mile races were an all-out challenge, then feeling a load of anxiety before attempting twice that distance was more than excusable. I was inexperienced, and it would be the first time I incorporated a support crew, each of which were inexperienced themselves with the sport of ultrarunning. I had to start somewhere, and this was it for me.

Packet pickup was a sharp reality check. As I stood in line to collect my bib, the race I was attempting the very next day began to finally resonate. I attended the race briefing, and the race director mentioned we should have a tail wind, which would actually make this an easy hundred. Making light of the distances we run brings excitement to the table and calms pre-race nerves. Talking with several veterans seemed to repeat some of the same advice, "Manage the heat and take things slow." I kept that at the very forefront of my mind. When I mentioned this was my first 100, they gave a chuckle and raised an eyebrow.

Could it be because only 55 percent of the individual 100-mile participants completed this race the previous year? The Keys100 website has a tips and frequently asked questions section that provides completion percentages. It states that the completion rate is almost entirely due to heat-related factors. It goes without saying that the distance is the additional factor, and the combination of the heat and humidity coupled with the distance made for a monster challenge. I would never know whether I'm capable of success unless I gave this one hell of an honest attempt.

After sleeping a couple of hours during the night, race morning arrived and the time had come. Everything was laid out and organized before, which made for a simple morning routine. I arrived at the starting line, and the waves of anxiety were unfaltering. Small quantities of runners were started in five-minute increments to help avoid traffic on Overseas Highway and alleviate crew-vehicle bombardments at checkpoints and aid-stations. My start time was 6:40 a.m., and when that time approached, reality sank in. I was moments away from starting my first 100-mile race. I crossed the starting line, and began decreasing the distance between myself and the finish. Each stride taken amounted to something, and every decision made from there on would inevitably affect the remaining portion of the race.

An enormous amount of self-awareness surrounded me. I was fortunate to run a race of this magnitude, and suddenly immense gratitude began to set in. I became mindful of attempting my ultimate goal. The miles clicked as I ran south, island hopping from one beautiful key to the next. Gigantic sea turtles and large stingrays skimmed the turquoise water's surface. These unique sightings kept me embedded within the present moment. Mindfulness and beautiful surroundings are moments that can't be duplicated, only remembered.

My goal was simply to finish this race, as I would suggest your goal be when you first attempt 100 miles. Between the fifty-mile and 100-mile distance, there is too much uncharted territory to accurately predict how the second half will likely unfold. Setting a time goal for your first 100 and failing to meet that specific demand can take away from the joy and satisfaction of finishing one of your greatest achievements. The combination of inexperience and the pressures of time can begin to impede on a memorable experience. However, if you feel determined to set a time goal, do not allow my advice or opinion to interfere.

This race has a thirty-two-hour cutoff, which relieves some pressure and makes finishing a possibility. Even though thirty-two hours seems like enough time, the blanket of heat and humidity that surrounds us can decrease the pace considerably. Additionally, time accrues during any breaks required to manage the heat and allow the body time to cool. The plan was to have my support crew meet up at mile twenty. In the meantime, Catherine and Christina would crew, as they knew my needs and routines from other previous ultras.

Catherine, roughly four months pregnant with Chase, had no issue with pacing duties from miles fifteen through twenty. Temperatures rose quickly, and began to flirt with ninety degrees Fahrenheit. Just as expected, my crew showed up around mile twenty, and made quite the entrance with a series of honks. David, Alioth, and Yoesly were hanging out of the sunroof and windows, six arms pumping straight in the air. Three people in the car, and six arms in the air confirms there were no hands on the all-important steering wheel. They were excited to see me, but my excitement was greater. The race was on, and this provided me with just the dose of adrenaline I needed. A fifth of the race was already completed, but the heat was beginning to catch up.

They jumped right in with the reorganization, pacing, and various crew duties necessary. Though unfamiliar with ultramarathons, my first-time crew consisted of friends who knew me and are physical therapists who know the body. This kind of knowledge and expertise can come in handy at extreme endurance events such as these. The overall excitement and surge of energy actually turned out to be pretty short lived. Soon after, I became increasingly nauseated from the intense heat and overall level of exertion. I had taken things slow and didn't do anything to deviate from my original plan. I stayed well within my slower pace, but I was nonetheless beginning to grow increasingly nauseated. An upset stomach, an ultrarunners worst nightmare, was slowly becoming my reality in an instant. My stomach was shot, and I had 75 percent of the distance left to cover.

Fear set in, as this was too early in the race to have a stomach already rejecting food and water. However, I had been in this position before, and had stubbornly fought through each and every time. After throwing up multiple times, I continued to progress down the Florida Keys, sipping just enough coconut water to get to the next checkpoint. I knew that coconut water not only rehydrates but offers some electrolytes with necessary calories. At this point in the race, if this was all my body could consume I would have nothing to complain about and had to keep moving. The vomiting would turn into dry heaves throughout the day, but I simply focused on continuing to move forward. The remainder of the day was filled with unsuccessful attempts to eat and drink. I just couldn't seem to hold down food or water, and knew it could take several hours for my stomach to resolve. In the meantime, I had to progress and keep moving at whatever pace possible. That way, when the issue resolved, I would at least have some distance behind me and a possible shot at still crossing the finish line.

The Keys 100 is not a race to have copious amounts of shade, but the unforgiving heat and exposure in the sun left most runners begging for it. I distinctly remember a brutal powerline section, where runners were lying in the slim shadow that each pole cast. Anything, it seemed, to hide from the heat and go for some shade. We rotated the crew for pacing duties, leaving two of them in the vehicle to leapfrog ahead. They prepared whatever was communicated forward via radio. Miles thirty through forty were harsh. Being dehydrated and exposed to the sun was beginning to catch up and slow me down drastically. Coming up on mile forty-two, a sign advertised the scorching section called Hell's Tunnel, a leg of the race that proved to be brutal and unforgiving. The sun was relentless, but so was I. The sunlight eventually began to lessen, and I began to feel physically restored and mentally rejuvenated. Around this time, another great friend of mine, Jose, joined up and began to pitch in. This only continued the trend that people believed in me and wanted to see me succeed.

Sipping the coconut water throughout the day had provided me enough energy to get from checkpoint to checkpoint. However, I was behind schedule from the number of breaks I required to cool down and manage the ongoing stomach issue. I was approaching the seven-mile bridge, which was part of the race that I was intimidated by the most. The situation I was currently faced with demanded a very ironic turning point in the race. I would have to do my best on arguably the toughest part of the course if I were to salvage any hope of finishing before thirty-two hours.

Catherine was pacing when we approached the fifty-three-mile mark, the last designated checkpoint before the seven-mile bridge. This was a designated crew location, followed by an aid-station at the other end of the bridge. The clock was applying some serious pressure, and I was really beginning to feel the stress. The crew vehicle was supposed to be waiting there, but they were absolutely nowhere to be found. Stressed out and unable to reach them over the radio, I was faced with having to make a serious decision. The choice was to move forward without any food or water or wait an unknown amount of time until the crew hopefully showed. To risk going alone without any supplies wasn't the absolute smartest idea, but waiting an unknown amount of time and sacrificing the race altogether wasn't an option either. I had given the day a maximum effort to stay within an inkling of hope, just to maintain the possibility of making it to the finish. It now felt like the entire race was on the line and boiled down to a miscommunication.

Just then, the crew showed up and pulled into the designated crew location. They explained that they missed the turn before the bridge, and once they drove onto it there was no way to turn around. This forced them to drive the entire seven-mile length of the bridge, just to be able to make a U-turn and head seven miles back. Yoesly told me there were dozens of runners still on the bridge, and many more of them were huddled at the mile-sixty aid-station. Knowing I wasn't in the struggle alone, it was then that I knew finishing was still within my grasp. I chose Yoesly, my training partner and running mentor, to take me through this particular segment of the race. He paced me those seven miles across the bridge, with zero access to any aid-stations, and where crew vehicle access is prohibited. This bridge is a one-way highway for the entire seven-mile stretch, with only a narrow shoulder of the bridge to run on. It was nighttime, and cars zipped by us at unrelenting speed.

I knew if I made up time on this particular stretch it could thrust me back into the possibility of finishing, and I would accomplish everything I had set out to achieve. Before the race even began, I knew that this segment would make or break me. Yoesly got me running a little more, and I began to grow a bit more assured. Wearing our headlamps, reflective vests, and blinking lights on the front and back, we ventured further into pitch-black darkness. No matter where I looked, I couldn't differentiate where the water's surface met the horizon or night sky. There was beauty in seeing how the runner's lights cast a multitude of colors with eye-catching luminance. I began to pass some that were crouched with their backs leaning against the hard cement barrier. My heart went out to them, as this was an unnerving location to hit the wall and crash

108

from feelings of energy depletion. I put a hand on their shoulders and asked if they needed anything. Most said no, and I continued onward. In a 100-mile race, no one chooses where they will hit the wall. If it happens to be in the middle of the seven-mile bridge, my prayers go out to you. At the center of the bridge, it's three-and-a-half miles to land in either direction. This is a portion that definitely needs to be strategized and planned for, and perhaps even done in non-stop fashion. I made up some time during that stretch, and eventually approached the mile-sixty aid-station. When I arrived, I didn't want to halt my momentum and decided to meet the crew a few miles further.

Throughout the night, I progressed when I could and at whatever pace possible. When combining the few hours of sleep the previous night and the day I had in the sun without eating, things were really beginning to catch up and take a toll. I laid down for about fifteen minutes at the next checkpoint, falling into what I call a half sleep. The body has absolutely had enough, but the mind was pumping a surplus of adrenaline. I was finally able to mentally recalibrate, and my body had its chance to recover for a few moments. I had some caffeine and got back on my feet. We alternated pacers through the rest of the night. Eventually, the early morning rays of the sun began to peek over the horizon. After going all day and all night, it revitalized my soul to see another sun rise.

Though I can't say my performance went well, I survived the day and even the night. Furthermore, I had ever so slowly inched my way closer and closer to the finish. After celebrating the sunrise with sky-high emotions, it was soon followed by a low dose of reality. The mile-marker sign reflected just enough light to see a number twenty come into view. Having only gone eighty miles, it became apparent this would be a fight to the end. It was an extremely rough day, which inevitably made for a very exhausting night. There remained a sizeable chunk of distance left to cover and, ironically, it felt the race had yet to begin.

Experiencing round two of the ninety-degree heat, especially feeling as weak as I did, only turned out to be the beginning of the race. I had to make up my mind then and there that, regardless of everything I had been working through, it wasn't enough of an excuse for failure. Quitting never crossed my mind, but I had to find a switch I never knew existed. I had to re-strategize, formulate a plan, and kick everyone into full throttle. When I arrived at each crew location, they swapped out hydration bottles, cooled me down with ice water, and swapped the rag from around my neck. I was grabbing pasta by the handful as my appetite finally came back with a vengeance. Going through my crew location was the closest I had ever felt to getting completely showered while strolling through a buffet.

This continued on until mile ninety-six, when I began telling Yoesly I needed a break. This is where a good pacer comes in, as he knew to lure me, little by little, to the next crew location at mile ninety-six and a half. I was literally on the verge of collapse, and was getting extremely close to lying down on the sidewalk. Somehow, he reeled me in another half mile where the safety of my crew and vehicle awaited. The only thing I called for was a chair, and when I finally approached it, I collapsed into it. It was a good push from mile eighty to ninety-six and a half, but, as I mentioned earlier, we don't have a choice where we might hit the wall. Only luck determines whether the location happens to be convenient or inconvenient.

I sat in the chair alongside the road, with only three-and-a-half miles between me and the finish. I was badly overheated, dehydrated, depleted of energy, and, despite the sleep deprivation, had made it to this point. Being so close to the finish did not necessarily make it any easier. There are simply no guarantees of success when it comes to running a race of these proportions. I have no idea what happened, but once I hit that chair and they applied ice water on my head, my body began to convulse in ways I've never experienced. Muscles were firing uncontrollably from hypersensitivity, probably from being extremely overheated and then being hit with ice water.

A relay team who had finished and was beginning to drive north saw this happen and stopped their van. All six of them began yelling at me and pumping their fists, holding down the horn with a series of honks, and screaming for me to get up and finish the race. There was enough noise at that moment to raise the dead. It worked, because although I couldn't speak or yell back, I pumped my fist back at them, and got my ass up and out of that chair. Over the next three-and-a-half miles, I began to feel better and tried to do some shuffling. I was nearing the finish line where my entire crew awaited and, as I approached, they all circled behind me. We all jogged together through the blue Keys 100 finishing chute.

Words cannot express the elation I felt as I jogged straight through that large finishing chute. When all odds had been against me since mile twenty-five, it was no reason to give in and feel sorry for myself. The race didn't go at all my way, but, as in life, we learn to roll with the punches. I finished in approximately thirty-one hours and twenty-seven minutes, with little more than thirty minutes left from cut-off. I am most impressed by this experience because of how much did not go in my favor. Despite the insurmountable odds that piled up against me, it is precisely what led me to finding my switch. At times it comes down to placing one foot in front of the other. All races will not go according to plan, but what we make of them will change us and define our experience. I was handed a Keys 100 belt buckle, and we all posed for one of my most meaningful pictures. A memory was captured in one single photo, but it was that moment when something inside me had changed. I experienced an unimaginable feeling of success, one that ultimately changed me forever.

CHAPTER 14:

Going the Ultra Mile

The Cross Florida 116

Nearly three years have passed since the Keys 100, due to the expansion of our family with the births of Chase and Connor. Though I ran a couple marathons and smaller ultras during that time, my mind was thinking of the day I would get another shot at the 100-mile distance. The Cross Florida 116 has always caught my attention because I thought it would be quite an experience to run across the state of Florida. I thought this distance was a bit more than my current capability, considering the fact that the Keys 100 wasn't the best race of my life. However, I had come a long way as a runner since then, and had gained a little more experience with ultrarunning. *Was I ready to attempt this race? Was I ready to run this distance?* There is absolutely no way of knowing unless I gave it an honest attempt.

I registered about eight months before the race, and was the first runner to sign up for the event. I began to officially train for it with six months to go. What I think some people don't realize is the investment of time and energy that goes into half a year of training. *Half a year of training for one particular race?* It can be a tremendous investment, but one that would be worth a tremendous amount of success and accomplishment. My focus was on volume, safely building up the weekly mileage as high as possible while placing emphasis on endurance aspects of strength training. I figured this would be the absolute best combination of training for this type of race. Given life's circumstances, which include traveling, the full-time job, and the large responsibility of parenting, I was able to ramp up to more than seventy miles a week prior to the race.

Training got to the point where I was waking up at three in the morning on Saturdays to get a marathon in before the family wakes. Multiple times per week I was waking up at four in the morning to run anywhere from ten to twelve miles before work. My wife and I had our system, alternating mornings between workouts and the morning responsibilities with our children. I was doing back-to-backs and even two-workout days during the same week, strength-training sessions, and even strengthening right before running. When it all comes together, confidence grows, and it becomes easier to place trust in the training we've endured.

A lot of planning is involved for a point-to-point race, in this case from the west coast of Florida, taking route forty all the way to the east coast of Ormond Beach. When traveling with a crew, there is a large amount of logistical planning. Hotels, a van rental, food, restaurants, hotels at the midway point for the parents and kids, and perhaps a few more hotels at the finish line. I kept monthly emails going out to all family and crew members with important details, directions, hotels, and race strategies. There is more that goes on behind the scenes than one would realize, aside from running the distance and executing a race plan. All for a shot to accomplish a race that I'm skeptical of whether it can even be achieved. I knew other runners have prevailed, but would I have the ability or mindset to?

For this crew, I recruited my brother Tony, who has gotten into marathons and ultras himself, and absolutely crushed his first marathon and 50K. David was returning to crew for his second time, which only proves he didn't learn his lesson the first time. A month before the race, we both ran the Miami Marathon side by side, which is such a rewarding experience to see someone gut out their first 26.2. Real friends are those who are with you from start to finish, not only in a race but through life in general. Chris was joining for his first time, but I never ask a single person to join if I don't think they have a special trait. Chris has every trait of a great friend and, needless to say, a great supportive crew member. He's intuitive about what needs to be done and can knock out a six-mile run without advance notice.

Catherine is a staple at every race, and having my wife present does a lot for me psychologically. She is a licensed mental health counselor (LMHC), so when I say she did some pacing, it means she probably snuck in some necessary therapy. She is another one who is capable of running whatever mileage necessary, and can help with either pacing or crew duties at the drop of a dime. In my opinion, there isn't a better combination of support for an ultrarunner. A group of physical therapists and a mental health counselor, what could possibly go wrong out there?

Yoesly moved out to the west coast of Florida, but eventually met up with us to crash the party. After scheduling to meet some friends for lunch in Saint Petersburg, we drove up to Crystal River where we would spend the night. My brother flew in from Georgia to help me knock out this race, and it was officially the first time I had my entire crew together. I briefed them on race strategies over dinner, and afterward showed them the gear in each and every bag. We called it a night; tomorrow was a big race.

I slept only a few hours the night before because Connor, then ten months old, woke up from time to time. Besides, the beds are never comfortable in the hotels we seem to trust before a race. Sleeping the night before a race is not nearly as important as sleeping well during the week leading up to the race. While running on little sleep the night before isn't the most ideal situation, as long as sleep deprivation doesn't accumulate over the stretch of time leading up to the race everything should be just fine in the end.

The start of the race begins at Bird Creek Boat Ramp in Yankeetown, Florida. The road that leads to the ramp itself is named Follow That Dream, after a 1962 film by the same name starring Elvis Presley. An appropriate name for the beginning of my journey. Not only was I the first runner to register, I was the first runner to arrive at the boat ramp. I was eager to begin, for that was what

I had been training for over the previous six months. As other runners arrived and the race director pulled in, I got out of the van to receive my bib number. In doing so, I immediately began to freeze. It was forty degrees Fahrenheit, but based on how the wind was blowing at that boat ramp the wind chill brought temperatures into the thirties.

It was nearing our starting time, so the opportunity to dip the toes in the Gulf of Mexico was now or never. We took some of the most beautiful pictures as the sunrise in the background shone purple and blue. My brother and wife watched me start, while the crew awaited at mile five. As we waited for our seven o'clock start time, I was talking with the race director who had run this race years earlier. The only thing he told me about this race was the emphasis he placed on the mental component. "This race is mentally tough," he stated very matter-of-factly, and with great emphasis on mentally tough. He said he's seen people drop at mile 100 and, to put it simply, it was not an easy race. My mindset was locked and loaded. I had prepared mentally for this race longer than I did physically. Five solo runners were attempting this race across the state of Florida, three men and two women. Out of curiosity, I'd done my research to see if I had the capabilities as the others registered. The only thing I found was that the two women who were running this race were extremely strong runners, and very experienced when compared to myself.

The race director counted down, and he started the race. My immediate strategy from the start was to run slower than the more experienced runners. If for whatever reason I was out in front of them, I am probably going to get myself in trouble. It turns out all four of them hung together for miles, and I made sure to run my race. My goal was to finish, as this was my first time attempting 116 miles, which must be completed within the thirty-two-hour cutoff. I wasn't concerned with the time, because I had a solid race plan and strategy in place. I would be concerned if my initial pace matched the two women. Their experience displayed even longer races and with even faster finishing times. If I could learn anything from them, it would be what pace I should not start this race. Over the next five miles, I began to lose sight of the only four runners attempting the full distance of the race.

I ran the first five miles with completely numb feet. I've always had the tendency to get colder than most, and in a much shorter span of time. I began to wonder whether or not I actually submerged my feet at the start. I knew my mind was already playing tricks, and began to steer my focus optimistically. I passed Bird Creek Bridge where Elvis Presley had fished and, lo and behold, there sat a fisherman with lines cast out. He tipped his cap good morning, and I gave him a nod. He was doing what he enjoyed, and I was doing what I enjoyed. I approached mile five, and was so happy to see all my friends and family. I didn't need anything from them, and told them to go another four or five miles. My strategy was to knock out the first fifteen miles, and then begin to work in some pacers. I couldn't have them sitting around getting bored, nor did I want them eating all my nutrition. I rotated them every five miles, starting with David to mile twenty, Chris up to mile twenty-five, then picking up my brother for the next five miles.

It didn't take long for my crew to get in sync and become a well-oiled machine. Our system operated like clockwork, and I could tell the race was falling into place. When I'm making good time and the effort seems effortless, it shows me the training, race plan, and execution are beginning to go as planned. Tony, my brother, and I cruised through miles twenty-five to thirty, and then swapped out with Catherine for the next five miles. I had been eating and drinking what I planned to, and everything unfolded no differently than it had during training. The crew vehicle awaited at mile thirty-five, and I communicated over the radio that I would take my first break. While running, I mentally strategize my needs, the order I will perform them, and try to calculate how long it may take. I was ready to eat some pasta with lentils, consume some water mixed with electrolytes, and knock out some stretching for the hips and lower leg. I wanted to break for precisely seven minutes, and was satisfied with the productivity during that time span.

Running the next couple of five-mile segments felt rejuvenating, but as I approached mile forty-five, I felt some hot spots beneath my feet. I communicated over the radio that I needed the chair, some tape, the scissors, and a new pair of socks. I wanted to keep this to a five-minute break. When I arrived everything was ready, and I sat down and pulled my shoes and socks off. I knew I didn't have blisters, but I also knew it was time to try and prevent them. This simple task can be taken care of in a five-minute span, but if I wait too long and the hot spots are ignored, it will eventually slow my overall pace. Blisters affect the running mechanics, and can lead to compensation, which eventually brings a slew of additional issues. I threw some tape on the hot spots, put on a new pair of socks, implemented some stretching, and was on my way. I was five miles away from mile fifty, which for me is a huge physical and mental milestone. My goal for mile fifty was to simply feel good when I eventually got there. *What good would it be if I completely trashed myself and didn't preserve anything for the remaining sixty-six miles?*

Chris paced me into mile fifty, and I hit both goals that I set out to accomplish. Not only did I arrive one hour ahead of schedule, but my goal was met in regard to feeling great. My time schedule was devised on the assumption I would finish in the thirty-two-hour cutoff. We were sitting at mile fifty, where my parents, kids, and support crew awaited, and they knew as well as I did the race was going well. It was also time for us to say our goodbyes, because the parents were taking Chase and Connor to the hotel in Ocala. I spent a fair amount of time with them while eating a burger and drinking a coffee. Simultaneously, we geared up for the night. It was eleven-and-a-half hours into the race, which put us at six-thirty p.m. The sun would set at seven p.m., just as we ventured through Ocala National Forest.

The temperature was nearing the low forties again, and just sitting there for ten minutes began to remind me I was cooling down. After eating a warm burger and drinking a hot coffee, it was time to head out and chip away at the night. We would continue our journey along route forty, and begin cutting straight through Ocala National Forest. It greeted us with a sign that shows bear crossing for the next thirty-three miles. Tony and I headed into the night with only our reflective vests, headlamps, and blinking lights visible.

Having a two-foot shoulder on the road to run on, route forty doesn't leave much room between you and passing vehicles traveling seventy to eighty miles per hour. The race website stated that if you had any issue with this, to go and run around Lake Okeechobee. Passing vehicles consisted of motorcycles, cars, and semi-tractor trailers. The big trucks and RVs have side mirrors sticking so far out, I actually had to step onto the grass in an attempt to keep my head intact. *Why not just run on the grass?* Much of it was uncut, at a serious sideways slope, making it tough to predict where the actual surface was. If I did that, it would be only a matter of time until I rolled an ankle or suffered from the effects of a gait deviation by running on a sideways slope for such a distance. I took my chances and ran on the pavement.

I had done some research on previous finishers and knew how to contact one of the runners who had actually accomplished this race crewed and uncrewed. I reached out to him, and we had a decent conversation about the race. He told me things to mentally prepare for, and running on the edge of the highway was one of them. I also tend to reach out to the race directors, introduce myself, and ask if there are any pointers they are willing to share regarding their race. Usually, anything they do offer can be of great help.

I changed up our strategy during the night, and wanted the van no more than a mile and a half ahead at any moment. At this point in the race things can happen pretty quickly, and I didn't want the van out of the radio's reception in the middle of Ocala National Forest. The temperature dropped to about forty-two degrees, but each car and truck that passed feet away from me brought an arctic blast of air upon my face. The trucks were big and the bikes were loud, but this kept me awake and alert during the long and tiresome run through the night. As the hours ticked by, I grew more and more tired. The more I ran, the more tired I became. The more I walked, the colder I felt. I ran to elevate my internal temperature, and walked to preserve my muscle strength.

I negotiated with myself that every six miles I would allow myself a five-minute break in the van, not only to heat up but to take a few minutes to relax and de-stress. When I got out, I started running to maintain the heat. The twelve hours of day forced me to hold back and exercise patience, and the twelve hours of night brought on a green light to push. The level of perceived exertion can change drastically, seemingly working twice as hard to go half as far. I reserved my strength and energy during the day to be able to give the night everything I had.

Yoesly showed up to the race at this point, and made an entrance with an entire RV. Though I didn't enjoy the RV's amenities, a water heater made it possible to enjoy a nice hot cup of tea. He paced me for a while, stretched me out afterward, and drove off to camp at a different location. It wasn't long after drinking the hot tea that I felt like I needed to use a bathroom. Running through Ocala National Forest in the middle of the night doesn't exactly offer convenience, at least not as far as bathrooms are concerned. In fact, you won't find anything but trees on both sides of route forty for thirty-three miles. Running wise, I had made a nice push during the day, and even throughout the night. But it was time to make the real push, and I knew it wasn't going to be easy. We communicated over the radio to get the toilet paper ready. Upon arrival, I grabbed the roll and went to handle some business. Sorry for the detail, but there is no ultramarathon without some fun and entertainment. I squatted up against a tree, my quads and hamstrings screaming at me due to the isometric position I had placed them in. My thigh muscles needed to hold me in place for as long as this was going to take.

Anyone who has held a squat against a wall in an isometric position knows it becomes increasingly difficult the longer the position is held for. Having to do this after running seventy miles made me wonder if this was karma's idea of a sarcastic joke. The bark from the tree was painfully digging against my back from the pressure I applied leaning up against it. As the beam of light from my headlamp shone downward, it appeared that large red ants were beginning to crawl up my shoes. This wasn't a bathroom break in peace, and I've never felt so pressured to do something that requires relaxation. It took pushing and yelling to find success, and now I had a support crew that was honestly scared to offer me any support. I was going to need a few minutes to recover.

Continuing to run throughout the night was getting tough. It was cold, and I was growing extremely tired; we were nowhere close to being done. It's important to ignore the totality of the race, for it could get overwhelming and difficult to fathom. Even a single mile will begin to look testing. But ironically, it's important to understand the totality of the race and continue to pace the mind to further endure. I mentally dismantle the race into psychologically manageable chunks of distance. I wasn't running 116 miles, and I wasn't even running six-mile segments until the break I negotiated with myself. I was running one-and-a-half miles at a time, not a mile more and not a mile less. Now somewhere along the line, the crew decided to venture just a tad beyond the one-and-a-half miles, for each time that small distance secretly added would accumulate over time and make a sizable difference. These are the kinds of decisions a great crew can make, as they know when to push me and when to back off.

It's important to mention that I had stopped concerning myself with what time it was and the distance I had run. I was ahead of schedule, and simply chose to stick with that thought. I knew the effort I had to maintain, and turned my focus to making it happen. Sleep deprivation and overall fatigue attempts to overthrow my determination, passion, and drive to succeed. The difficulty continued to creep from behind, and felt like a continuous nip at my heels. I kept my meaning and purpose at the forefront of my mind, as this race required constant mental focus. Cross Florida was becoming the challenge I had sought.

The pain my body was beginning to endure is only expected when running long distances. There will be an element of pain involved, and having that level of acceptance beforehand begins to develop a lack of reaction to it. Sleep deprivation is no surprise, and despite only sleeping a couple hours the previous night, I managed to get through this race on only twenty seconds of sleep. That twenty seconds of sleep happened to come, undecided, when I leaned against a pole to take a leak. I leaned my body against the pole and laid my head upon the sign. I fell asleep in that position and woke up when I finished. I then resumed my running again.

Wildcat Lake was mile seventy-eight and a half, and it was said to possibly have an aid-station. I didn't know what mile I was on until I heard a shout coming from across the highway. There was a table, topped with various things a runner might need, and a kerosene lantern offering a bit of light. The previous race director stood there in the cold. He offered a hot cup of coffee, which was all it took to turn my entire night around. This race just blew my mind. Out in the middle of Ocala National Forest, standing there in forty-two-degree weather, was someone waiting to see if I may need or want anything. *How selfless is that?* He was waiting for me. The two women were about an hour or so ahead, and the other two men had dropped out of the race before nightfall. That selflessness exists in the ultrarunning community just to see someone achieve their goals and accomplish something extraordinary.

I walked the rest of the way to where the crew vehicle waited, so I could sip this hot cup of coffee I worked so hard for. I climbed into the van at mile eighty, and Tony and David looked extremely confused. I told them I met a guy named George Maxwell (the previous race director) along the way, and he handed me this big hot cup of coffee. It was approximately four a.m., it was still pitch black, and I was in the middle of nowhere. I can understand their confusion, perhaps with a little hint of jealousy. After all, I was raving about how great the coffee was and don't recall ever offering them any.

I was so engrossed in this mental battle that not even an imaginary crowbar could have pried me from it. I played a thousand mind games against the race, and it had a thousand mind games waiting for me. It was a constant, non-stop psychological battle. From my preliminary training perspective, that is why the mindset should be set in place initially. The race frequently contains mentally fatiguing variables, and we must be diligently prepared to retaliate with equally strong countermeasures. So, when the race is trying to deplete our fortitude, directing the mind to optimistic outcomes can begin to preserve our mental strength.

Psychologically, it can largely depend on what it is I choose to focus on. If I am growing fatigued from the trucks, cars, and bikes whizzing by me, the race will inevitably continue to mentally fatigue me from that perspective. If I am hyper focused on the pain, it may only begin to exacerbate the feeling, and psychologically continue to fatigue me from that perspective. A certain degree will depend on what we place our focus on. It depends on the direction our mindset is being steered and, the deeper we get into these races, the more important that concept will become. It is going to be exhausting and painful, and will be physically, mentally, and emotionally taxing. We should expect the breakthrough of perceived limitations to be opportunistic, but nothing short of feeling outright difficult. The majority of the outcome can depend on many variables, but the direction of our mindset is one within our control. A positive mental outlook during the toughest of times can help offset some of the conditions against us. Physically speaking, my body only continued to break down. After all, my furthest training run before this race was a twelve-hour timed event, and I targeted a bit more than fifty miles in that timeframe. Completing this race would require me to run another sixty-six miles on top of the fifty, so I expected that this event would be very physically taxing. For obvious reasons, we cannot fully rely on the physical body, therefore our vantage point has now become psychological. We have choices about where we place our mindset, and depending on the directions we veer in, whether positive or negative, can influence the flow and outcome of the overall race. If we continue down a negative path, we are only playing for our opponents, in which case the race has the overall advantage. Staying positive the majority of the time can keep our heads in the game and level the playing field.

Emotionally speaking, it can be the familiar equivalent of a roller-coaster ride. When exploring what is beyond our breaking points, we are placing ourselves in a very vulnerable state. Time applies massive amounts of pressure throughout the race, whether it is the cutoff or the time goals we place on ourselves, the clock rides us from the very start. The race can also become stressful at times, as waves of extreme highs and lows flood inward. The longer the duration of the race, the higher the highs and lower the lows. Feelings of standing on top of the world and the world crashing down upon us are temporary, and tend to come and go, more or less, as they please.

Hopping in the van once again, the crew asked me if I wanted to know the progress I had made. Having ignored my watch for the majority of the night, I wondered whether I'd fallen behind or managed to keep pace. It was mile ninety and nearing six-thirty a.m., and I was twenty-three hours into the race. Tears of joy were too strong to hide, so I sat there to embrace the elation I felt. All that I'd been through to get to this point made hearing this news motivational and invigorating. I took a nice ten-minute break to relax and let the emotions settle. I then jumped out of the van and ran the next mile and a half straight. I ran that next segment and didn't let up, but it was the last time during the race that I ran so smoothly.

Mile ninety was a great mental milestone, knowing I had about a marathon to go. Though I do not focus on the remaining distance, I do have mental checkpoints and feel rejuvenated when I scratch them off my list. I also knew in the back of my mind that the race had yet to begin. The timing couldn't be any more perfect for a second sunrise to make an appearance. The exuberance from the news of reaching mile ninety in twenty-three hours, the second sunrise, and then reaching mile one hundred felt like a grand slam. As I arrived at the hundred-mile check point, the crew awaited outside the van along with Rich, the race director. They all welcomed me to the hundredth mile. It was gratifying to see the race director, so we talked a moment before I moved on. There was still a lot of distance left to cover, and he yelled as I was leaving, "Only sixteen miles left, an easy sixteen." We make light of the distances we run, and it reminds me to bring laughter to a situation that warrants optimism.

It was twenty-five-and-a-half hours into the race when I arrived at the hundred-mile checkpoint. My goal was to feel like I had more in the tank, because it felt like the race was only beginning. Everyone looked forward to the sunrise, and I think everyone was looking forward to crossing that hundred-mile mark. We were all delirious, to say the least, so I told them I wasn't letting my guard down. Though this point could have called for a worthy celebration, it wasn't time for all that just yet. I had learned from my basketball days never to celebrate too early.

My whole family met up at mile 103, and it was nice to see both of my boys again. I sipped some hot coffee, and it was time to get moving again. Arriving at mile 107 ½, I needed to change my socks and apply more tape on the bottoms my feet. Some may think tending to an issue at this point in the race is meaningless, but I beg to differ. Anything can happen at any moment, and I don't need potential problems beginning to stack up. I had come too far to change up my strategy. Nothing was guaranteed until I cross that finish line. Until then, I had work to do.

It was a long and tough walk, and I couldn't seem to get the legs turning over into a jog. I walked the remaining portion of the race until I got to the I-95 underpass, which signified the approach to Ormond Beach. From mile 100, we had counted our one-and-a-half-mile segments, and were under the impression we had gone 114 miles. I overheard Chris on the radio mention we still had another six to go. I asked David if that was what I heard, but he ignored me and said I had heard wrong. The thought continued to ferment and, knowing the fragile state I was in at this point of the race, it was important for me to know the difference. I needed to know if I had two more miles or another six for the sake of the race. We had tracked our progress from the hundredth mile, and knew roughly two more miles remained at this point. Mentally, it was a big difference if I had to run six more miles instead of two. Catherine told me it was six and I was instantly crushed. I thought this race started at the 100, but that was my incorrect assumption. My invisible starting line was the I-95 underpass, with six more miles to go.

It felt like the hammer finally came down on me. It was at that point, the I-95 underpass heading toward Ormond Beach, where I was physically, mentally, and emotionally depleted. I shed a few tears and walked faster, filled with anger. It then began to rain, a symbolic mockery of my attempt to cross the state of Florida. Mentally, I went to a place where nothing in my life was able to pin me down, and this race was not going to be the first. This was the moment when mind and heart prevailed. Breaking through barrier after barrier prepared me for this moment in time, and I continued to press forward with passion, power, and sheer determination. I was strictly business, and wanted this done. I was excited to start and now found myself anxious to finish. The very last mile consisted of a large, high bridge, crossing over a body of water right before the coast. I powered my way up the bridge quickly, and became replenished with energy as the coast came in to view. It removed any inkling of pain I'd been feeling, and suddenly I was filled with elation.

The whole crew waited at the base of the bridge, and we walked together another three blocks to the finish. Signs and posters welcomed me in, and the race director stood at the official endpoint. I celebrated heavily as I got to the finish, and Rich said my time was thirty-one hours and eleven minutes. We cheered, and I shook his hand while being congratulated. I was happy to have run his race, and he was happy to see me complete it. The same emotion, but for completely different reasons. He told me to walk across the street and dip my toes in the Atlantic Ocean. We were on the other side of Florida, and a quick thought passed over me. *How the hell did we get here?* The race veteran I spoke with before this race told me that crossing the state and getting to the other side was a feeling I didn't want to miss. He was right. Running coast to coast was the type of feeling that will never be forgotten, nor can it be explained. Coast to coast, and everything in between.

As I walked across the street with the crew and family, someone asked him what was up with the extra mileage. His response was plain and simple, "Those are called Ultra Miles!" We all laughed about that, and the beach was within a couple hundred feet. It was a cold day, but I didn't care. I had visualized myself running into the Atlantic since the moment I had first registered eight months earlier. The time had arrived to make that visualization a reality. I took off running, and experienced a wide array of emotions: gratitude, happiness, and realization of how lucky I was to accomplish something I didn't think was possible. To have all the love and support from start to finish, for all thirty-one hours and eleven minutes, is a gift that's become hard to repay.

My feet and legs hit the Atlantic Ocean, and that was one of the best finish lines I've ever experienced. I cannot thank my support crew enough for being by my side from start to finish. I always send an email afterward to thank the race director for putting on a great race and for playing a part in my overall journey. When I thanked him, he replied with an email thanking me. It occurred to me that, since the feeling was mutual, we all inspire one another in many different ways. As for the two women who ran ahead of me the entire race, kudos to you two for running it together in an astounding twenty-eight hours and twenty-eight minutes. You two are a testament of how strong women are in the sport of ultrarunning, and I wish you the very best on your future endeavors.

Hugging everyone on the beach after my celebratory run is one of the greatest moments in my life, and largely because I had both Chase and Connor present. That moment made every minute of training and running this race worth the success and overall achievement. There are many reasons I run ultramarathons.

The moments to share, the success to pursue.

To expand my horizons and seek endless possibility.

To explore the unbounding of all limitations, with every goal I set and every race that I run.

I run to feel free, and for the freedom to run far.

I run for the infinite challenges this sport has to offer.

Mainly, I run for the opportunity to put one foot in front of the other, and to be able to ultimately go the Ultra Mile.

To be continued …